WALKING A THINLINE

WALKING A THIN LINE

ANOREXIA
&
BULIMIA

The Battle Can Be Won!

PAM VREDEVELT
JOYCE WHITMAN

MULTNOMAH · PRESS

Portland, Oregon 97266

Unless otherwise indicated, all Scripture quotations are from the Holy Bible: New International Version, copyright 1978 by the International Bible Society. Used by permission of Zondervan Bible Publishers.

Scripture references marked NASB are from the New American Standard Bible, © The Lockman Foundation 1960, 1962, 1963, 1968, 1971, 1972, 1973, 1975, 1977.

Verses marked *Phillips* are taken from J. B. Phillips: *The New Testament in Modern English*, revised edition. © J. B. Phillips 1958, 1960, 1972.

Verses marked Amplified Bible are from The Amplified New Testament, copyright 1954, 1958 by The Lockman Foundation.

Verses marked TLB are taken from The Living Bible, © 1971 by Tyndale House Publishers, Wheaton, Ill.

Cover design by Al Mendenhall/Judy Quinn
Edited by Liz Heaney

WALKING A THIN LINE: Anorexia and Bulimia, the Battle Can Be Won
© 1985 by Multnomah Press
Printed in the United States of America

Library of Congress Cataloging-in-Publication Data

Vredevelt, Pam W., 1955-
   Walking a thin line.

   Bibliography: p.
      1.Anorexia nervosa.   2. Bulimarexia.
I. Whitman, Joyce R. (Joyce Rasdall), 1952-
II. Title.
RC552.A5V74   1985   616.85'2   85-18916
ISBN 0-88070-117-X

85   86   87   88   89   90   –   10   9   8   7   6   5   4   3   2   1

CONTENTS

FOREWORD

During the past decade the epidemic problem of eating disorders has captured the attention of our country. The awareness has resulted in concern and an increased effort to find help for those who struggle and suffer with eating disorders.

I am encouraged and delighted with this highly informative and solution-oriented book. Its contents are clearly stated for the average layperson and will be helpful not only for the individual who has an eating disorder, but also for family members and friends. This book also needs to be shared with those who have no association with this problem so that they will be able to identify anorexia or bulimia when they see it as well as give help and encouragement.

I hope this book will encourage those with either anorexia or bulimia to seek the professional help which is needed.

H. Norman Wright
Director, Family Counseling and Enrichment
Christian Marriage Enrichment

ACKNOWLEDGMENTS

We would like to give special thanks to:

Christ and His church, where strugglers find hope and rest.

To our friends who encouraged us in writing.

Norm Wright, Kim Lampson, Lynn Bissonette, and Cherry Boone O'Neill—other experts who have inspired us and contributed to our approach.

Betty Gussey, our faithful typist, who knows each page of this book as well as we do.

Liz Heaney and Multnomah Press for their sensitivity to the need for tools in resolving eating disorders.

READ THIS FIRST!

To the ignorant, an eating disorder is something that people should just "snap out of."

To the curious, an eating disorder only afflicts people who are neurotic.

To Christians, an eating disorder is something that happens to non-Christians.

To most people, an eating disorder is confusing—and we'd rather not think about it.

But to those with anorexia nervosa or bulimia, it is a life-threatening problem. The sight of food assaults the senses and unleashes a flood of memories of failure, pain, and conflict. It is a reminder of shattering defeats and triggers doubts about the victim's competency to ever gain control of life. The person struggling with anorexia or bulimia is obsessed with his disorder and is often unable to escape the tightening chains of its destructive grasp. Sometimes this compulsive behavior can lead to death.

What follows is an attempt to extend a lifeline to those with eating disorders. *This book is not intended to act as a substitute for professional help.* Instead, it is intended to offer tools to those who are suffering. It is designed to turn on a light for those who are "in the closet" and to give assurance that the battle can be won. It is written to give information and support to the family and friends of those who struggle. They, too, encounter difficult challenges. And finally, it is written for the professional counselor as a resource for clients who desire to use both psychological and biblical tools in the process of restoration.

For several years we have counseled with many people caught in the vise of anorexia and/or bulimia. They have been some of the most challenging years of our lives. As therapists, it has driven us into an intensive study of research available on eating disorders. As individuals, it has driven us to our knees and into God's Word, the Bible, to search for answers and hope for our clients.

We have written this book over a two year period during which we have both been consistently working with eating disorder victims. As associate therapists, we felt there was a tremendous need for a book that offered practical tools for overcoming anorexia and bulimia from a Christian perspective.

We have chosen to write in first person throughout the book because it is simpler and smoother stylistically and because our approach to treatment is the same.

Although both men and women are victims of eating disorders, we have targeted women as the audience for this book. Joyce was responsible for the content in chapters 4, 8, 9, 10, and 14. Pam authored the remaining chapters and stylized the writing of the book to give it continuity and flow.

We are not writing about coping with eating disorders from a strictly theological position—although we believe Jesus Christ is the Son of God, the One who died on the cross and rose again from the dead as a sacrifice for our sins. We are enthusiastically involved in an ongoing personal relationship with God and we're convinced that He is the Great Healer . . . the One we can depend on for power and strength to win life's battles and to cope with life's problems.

In the following pages you will read about some of the factors that contribute to anorexic and bulimic behavior. We want to tell you some honest and transparent stories that have evolved in sessions with some of our clients who have graciously offered to give you an inside peek into the private areas of their lives. Although details have been changed to provide anonymity, you will sense their pain and anguish. You will see that they are individuals much like you . . . ones with jobs, families, and church and social involvements. You will also feel their joy and wonder in new beginnings and sense their newfound freedom.

Perhaps you will find stories similar to your own experiences in the chapters that follow. Let us encourage you to face head on whatever surfaces. One way to do that is to record your thoughts, feelings, and insights concerning your disorder in a notebook. You may want to call it your Personal Growth Notebook. As you read, have your notebook handy so that you can use it to answer questions, take notes, or express your innermost thoughts. Seeing your thoughts and feelings in black and white can be very helpful. Your perspectives will become clearer and you will also have a concrete point of reference from which to evaluate your growth.

Our prayer and the prayer of our clients is that you will gain personal insight and understanding from the stories that are shared. A friend of ours once said, "Some people are readers and some people are grabbers." We're praying that you will be a grabber . . . that every tool or insight you glean from these pages will become a part of you. And as you grab, we're asking God for His healing work in you to move you from "glory to glory" and from strength to strength.

Pam & Joyce

PART
1

BEGINNING
THE SEARCH
FOR ANSWERS

THE EATING DISORDER EPIDEMIC: WHO ARE THE CASUALTIES?

"How come you didn't tell everyone about the benefits of an eating disorder?" she asked, shaking my hand. I had just spent two hours discussing anorexia nervosa and bulimia and the devastating effects they have on their victims.

"I'm not sure I understand your question," I said.

"Eating disorders aren't all bad, and they don't always end in tragedy and disappointment. Look at me. I've been bulimic for sixteen years, feel fine, and still have my size five figure at age thirty-six. Can I take you to lunch?"

While driving to the restaurant, I learned that this attractive, polished woman was a mother of two children and was responsible for leading the large college department at her church.

"I think your statistic that one in five college women are bulimic is very conservative," she said. "Most of the good-looking girls in my college group vomit every day. How else can we eat pizza, go to potlucks and church activities, and not get fat? After all, the Romans used to do it as a regular custom at their feasts. The idea isn't new."

"When did your bulimia begin?"

"When I was twenty, I wore a size twelve dress. I was sitting around the dinner table with some friends in the college cafeteria and somehow we got on to the subject of dress size. We were comparing facts and figures when it dawned on me that I wore the largest size. I remember swallowing that last bite of dessert with tremendous guilt and thinking, 'I've got to find a way to wear less than a size twelve.'

"The next day I found my escape. It was a sorority tradition to go out for pizza at 10:00 P.M. every Thursday night. Six of us devoured three giant pizzas in less than thirty minutes. One of my sorority sisters sitting across from me stood to go to the women's room and mumbled under her breath, 'I've got to get rid of this.' I was confused by her statement, but passed it off. I decided to use the restroom before leaving. As I pushed open the swinging door, I heard someone heaving in the first stall. I was just about to knock and ask if I could do anything to help, when my sorority sister walked out. With a sigh of relief she said, 'I feel so much better now.'

"I had always wondered how she could eat like a horse and retain her petite figure. Now I knew. Excitement swelled inside me as I thought about this great solution. I could eat whatever I wanted and leave my size twelves in my past."

"Have you ever thought about trying another form of weight control?" I asked gently.

"What? You must be kidding! Give up my size five figure? Give up delicious food? Why would I ever want to do that?"

THE M.I.T. GRADUATE

She was a dazzling blonde with bright blue eyes. We met after a seminar I had given at a local athletic club. Immaculately dressed, she looked as if she modeled for *Vogue* magazine. She asked if I had a minute to listen.

The checkered history of her life seemed to focus on one complaint: "I want so much to be the best at everything I do. I need to feel like I'm really excelling or else life isn't worth living. Everyone is drawn to winners, but it's hard to win all the time and always to be the best."

Carol was an M.I.T. graduate with a 4.0 GPA. She was well known in her city, successful in business, and highly regarded for her leadership abilities and achievements.

"Have you been struggling with an eating disorder?" I asked. She flinched, looked at the floor, and hesitantly nodded. "Can you tell me about it?"

"I never intended for it to go this far. In college I used laxatives maybe once a week after a eating a lot. But now it's every day, and I'm trapped. I can't quit, and I'm scared to death that it's going to end up killing me."

As the tears streamed down her face, she cried, "I feel like such a loser. I've done everything I know to stop, but I'm hooked."

THE HIGH SCHOOL FRESHMAN

I was scrubbing the oven when there was an unexpected knock at the front door. Sherilee stood on the step with trouble written all over her face.

As we sat at the kitchen table, I began to catch a glimpse of some of the pain and turmoil she was experiencing. That morning her parents had told her that if she didn't start eating, they were going to hospitalize her. She couldn't understand how they could be so cruel. Sobbing angrily, she cried, "I hate them when they try to push me around like that! Why don't they get off my back and just leave me alone?"

Treading lightly, I asked, "How long has it been since you have eaten?"

"Only twelve days. Some of my friends starve themselves two to three weeks. Besides, I'm not hungry."

"How is your energy level, Sherilee?"

"It's fine. I drink diet coke all day, or coffee, and I'm never tired. I don't even want to sleep at night. I have so much energy; I don't know why Mom and Dad are making such a big deal out of this."

"How long were you planning to starve yourself?"

"Only two weeks. Rally tryouts are next week and I've got to be skinny by then. They never pick fat cheerleaders. I've just got to lose the weight I gained over the summer. There's no other way except to quit eating.

"I've asked God to take off the pounds and give me the desire to eat if He wanted me to stop starving. I have no desire to eat, so what I'm doing must be O.K. with God."

DEFENDER OF THE CAUSE

I had just finished a seminar on eating disorders. Stimulating questions had been asked in the discussion time. Many had been eager to learn how to help themselves or others imprisoned by eating disorders.

A university student cornered me by the coffee table and expressed her anger about the approaches professionals were taking in their treatment of anorexia nervosa and bulimia. Coming right to the point, she said, "You call it an eating disorder; I call it weight control. You call it a serious problem; I call it an effective tool. There are thousands of diet aids and diet tools on the market. Self-starvation and purging just happen to be inexpensive and effective ways to control weight gain. You're just like the rest of the diet pushers—trying to make a dollar by discussing people's insecurities about fat." She made a quick 180 degree turn and walked out.

THE PAPER MILL WORKER

Greg picked up a cup of coffee, thinking it would help him get out of his stupor. He had consumed twelve Danish pastries on the way to work. His throbbing headache and sour stomach put him on edge. When his partner walked over to his post and accidentally dropped a steel bar on the cement, Greg hurled his scalding hot coffee across the room, screaming, "Why do you have to be so clumsy?" Embarrassment and anger welled up inside him as he realized what he had done. "How stupid can you get, Greg? You're a nervous wreck and a stupid idiot . . . a good-for-nothing jerk!"

Throughout the rest of the day, Greg continued to torment himself by engaging in full-blown binges and numerous forced vomitings. He told himself, "You'll never get a decent job outside of this run-down factory. You'll never change because you're a failure. What's the use of living if this is all there is to life?"

Greg had been bulimic for thirteen years. His eating disorder began in high school when he vomited occasionally to keep his weight down during wrestling season. Straining to make the 132 pound limit—more than 15 pounds below his normal weight—Greg would sometimes shed 6 pounds in the twenty-four hours before a meet. Wearing a rubberized suit, he would jump rope for two hours a night, and then stagger upstairs to keep the sweat flowing and plunge into a piping-hot bath tub. His food intake for the day before a meet usually consisted of an apple and one cup of yogurt. Following his matches, he gorged on pizza and junk food with the guys and then purged by vomiting or laxative abuse. The vomiting was easy for him and gradually became a daily part of his routine. He was convinced he had found the answer to staying trim, so he continued to control his weight by starving, bingeing, and purging. But his strategy backfired.

When Greg first came in for counseling, he was serious about ending his life. His method of suicide was well planned, his intentions obvious. His fear that as a Christian he might not go to heaven if he took his own life was all that kept him from taking action. I listened as he talked about his feelings of despair and panic.

During the months that followed, Greg began to acknowledge and understand his feelings and behavior. After six months of counseling, his binges ceased, and his violent emotional outbursts ended. He had learned new ways to manage anger and worked hard at applying his new coping strategies.

EATING DISORDERS ON THE RISE

These are just five of the many people who have shared their eating secrets with me—mothers, pastor's wives, counselors, men, church members, professionals, and outstanding leaders. They represent the increasing number of men and women afflicted with an eating disorder.

This evening I viewed a televised documentary about a teenager, Carrie, who was hooked into a destructive lifestyle of self-starvation. The final scene showed Carrie's parents standing arm in arm over her grave site. They were stunned. Their fifteen-year-old daughter had gone from 120 pounds to 70 pounds in just five months. Her energetic body had been reduced to bone and organs functioning solely by artificial life machines . . . and now she was dead. All this for the sake of thinness.

New York psychotherapist Steven Levenkron, who has treated anorexic patients for the last ten years, states some startling facts about anorexia nervosa:

- There are approximately 80,000 reported cases nationally.[1]
- Approximately ninety percent of anorexics are female, and the disorder often strikes at puberty.[2]
- Anorexia has a mortality rate of up to twenty-two percent.[3]

A wave of grief spread among the fans of musician Karen Carpenter, February 4, 1983. While searching her closet for something to wear for the day, Karen collapsed to the floor. As paramedics anxiously administered help, she went into cardiac arrest. Despite the continuous efforts of professionals to resuscitate her, Karen was pronounced dead at the hospital. Dead at thirty-two! She was a victim of anorexia nervosa.

Carrie and Karen are not the only people who have fallen prey to the entangling chains of this disease. A recent survey across America showed that one of ten women between the ages of twelve and thirty-five struggle with anorexia nervosa or bulimia.[4] These are findings based on documented cases. Those in the medical profession feel it is safe to assume that there are at

27

least as many or more "in-the-closet" victims as there are those who are seeking professional help.

Consider these additional facts:

- Today more than fifty percent of American girls have been on a reducing diet before completing adolescence.[5]
- For every one hundred women suffering from anorexia or bulimia, there are five to ten men, and for every person that is anorexic, twelve are bulimic.[6]
- Approximately 7,600,000 women and 380,000 men in America would test out as bulimic.[7]
- Sixty percent of all models and ballerinas have eating disorders. It is predicted that from one to three percent of the female population will have anorexia or bulimia at one time in their life.[8]
- A high incidence of eating disorders is found among serious athletes. Dr. Charles Tipton, professor in the department of physical education, physiology, and biophysics at the University of Iowa, says that in a study of 582 wrestlers who were certified for competition, he found that on the average seven to eight pounds were lost the day prior to a match. "The weight slash came as a result of rigid exercise, strict food deprivation, fluid restriction, and exercising in a hot environment. Dehydration is by far the quickest and probably the most frequently used method of weight loss. Food deprivation is second."[9]
- Before defecting to the U.S. in 1981, Bela Karolyi was head coach of Romania's

gymnastic team and mentor to its star performer in the 1976 Olympics, Nadia Comaneci. Nadia's slight build—five feet, eighty-six pounds—and her stunning performance at the Olympics established her slim physique as the ideal for gymnasts. Karolyi says, "Too many coaches are forcing athletes into severe diets. As a result, athletes who have a difficult time with rigidly controlled dieting are resorting to self-starvation, induced vomiting, and laxatives."[10]

WHAT ARE THE SYMPTOMS OF ANOREXIA NERVOSA AND BULIMIA?

Both anorexia nervosa and bulimia are characterized by a compulsive urge to control weight. Very simply, *anorexia nervosa* is self-induced starvation resulting in extreme weight loss. *Bulimia* can be easily understood as a pattern of bingeing (eating large amounts of food) followed by self-induced vomiting or laxative abuse—with or without weight loss. Here is a list of some key symptoms of both eating disorders.

ANOREXIA NERVOSA	BULIMIA
Voluntary starvation often leading to emaciation and sometimes death.	The binge-purge syndrome.
	Person is usually within ten or fifteen pounds of ideal body weight.
Rigid dieting is the sole cause of dramatic weight loss. No underlying medical reasons.	Secretive binge eating. Can occur regularly and may follow a pattern. Caloric intake per binge can range from 1,000 to 20,000 calories.[11]

Occasional binges followed by fasting, laxative abuse or self-induced starvation.

Binges are followed by fasting, laxative abuse, self-induced vomiting, or other forms of purging. Person may chew food but spit it out before swallowing.

Menstrual period ceases. May not begin if anorexia occurs before puberty.

Menstrual periods may be regular, irregular, or absent.

Excessive exercise.

Swollen glands in neck beneath jaw.

Hands, feet, and other parts of the body are always cold.

Dental cavities and loss of tooth enamel.

Dry skin. Head hair may thin, but downy fuzz can appear on other parts of the body.

Broken blood vessels in face. Bags under eyes.

Depression, irritability, deceitfulness, guilt, and self-loathing.

Fainting spells. Rapid or irregular heartbeat.

Thinks "I'm much too fat" even when emaciated.

Miscellaneous stomach and intestinal discomforts and problems.

Obsessive interest in food, recipes, and cooking.

Weight may often fluctuate because of alternating periods of bingeing and fasting.

Rituals involving food, exercise, and other aspects of life.

Perfectionistic.

Introverted and withdrawn. Avoids people.

Wants relationships and approval of others.

Maintains rigid control.   Loses control and fears she cannot stop once she begins eating.

RATING YOUR TENDENCIES

Anorexia nervosa and bulimia are life-threatening compulsions. If you are anorexic or bulimic, you need to get help as soon as possible. If several of the above symptoms are a part of your lifestyle, you may have an eating disorder. In order to gain further insight, you may wish to take the time to fill out the following questionnaire. This test is not intended to be a diagnostic assessment, but it can help you identify the strength of your anorexic or bulimic tendencies.

DYING TO BE THIN QUESTIONNAIRE*

Answer the following questions honestly. Write the number of your answer in the space at the left.

—————1. I have eating habits that are different from those of my family and friends.
1) Often 2) Sometimes 3) Rarely 4) Never

—————2. I find myself panicking for fear of gaining weight if I cannot exercise as I planned.
1) Almost always 2) Sometimes 3)Rarely 4) Never

—————3. My friends tell me I am thin, but I don't believe them because I feel fat.
1) Often 2) Sometimes 3) Rarely 4) Never

—————4. My menstrual period has ceased or become irregular due to no known medical reasons.
1) True   2) False

—————5. I have become obsessed with food to the point that I cannot go through a day without worrying about what I will or will not eat.

1) Almost always 2) Sometimes 3) Rarely 4) Never

—————6. I have lost more than twenty-five percent of the normal weight for my height. (For example, you weigh 120 lbs. and lose 30 lbs.)

1) True   2) False

—————7. I would panic if I got on the scale and found I had gained two pounds.

1) Almost always 2) Sometimes 3) Rarely 4) Never

—————8. I find that I prefer to eat alone or when I am sure no one will see me. Then I can make excuses so I can eat less and less with friends and family.

1) Often 2) Sometimes 3) Rarely 4) Never

—————9. I find myself going on uncontrollable eating binges during which I consume large amounts of food to the point that I feel sick and make myself vomit.

1) 3 or more times per day 2) 1-2 times per day 3) 1-2 times per week 4) Rarely 5) Never

—————10. I use laxatives as a means of weight control.

1) On a regular basis 2) Sometimes 3) Rarely 4) Never

—————11. I find myself playing games with food. (Example: cutting it up into tiny pieces, hiding food so people will think I ate it, chewing it and spitting it out without

swallowing, or telling myself certain foods are bad.)
1) Often 2) Sometimes 3) Rarely 4) Never

————12. People around me have become very interested in what I eat, and I find myself getting angry at them for pushing food on me.
1) Often 2) Sometimes 3) Rarely 4) Never

————13. I have felt more depressed and irritable than I used to, and/or have been spending increasing amounts of time alone.
1) True   2) False

————14. I keep a lot of my fears about food and eating to myself because I am afraid no one would understand.
1) Often 2) Sometimes 3) Rarely 4) Never

————15. I enjoy making gourmet, high-calorie meals or treats for others as long as I don't have to eat any myself.
1) Often 2) Sometimes 3) Rarely 4) Never

————16. The most powerful fear in my life is the fear of gaining weight or becoming fat.
1) Often 2) Sometimes 3) Rarely 4) Never

————17. I find myself totally absorbed when reading books about dieting, exercising, and calorie counting to the point that I spend hours studying them.
1) Often 2) Sometimes 3) Rarely 4)Never

————18. I tend to be a perfectionist and am not satisfied with myself unless I do things perfectly.
1) Almost always 2) Sometimes 3) Rarely 4) Never

————19. I go through long periods of time

without eating anything (fasting) as a means of weight control.
1) Often 2) Sometimes 3) Rarely 4) Never

—————20. It is important to me to try to be thinner than all of my friends.
1) Almost always 2) Sometimes 3) Rarely 4) Never

Add your score together and compare with the table below:

Under 30 Strong tendencies toward anorexia nervosa
30-45 Strong tendencies toward bulimia
45-55 Weight conscious, not necessarily with anorexic or bulimic tendencies
Over 55 No need for concern

*© 1982 by K. Kim Lampson. Used by permission.

If you scored below 45, it would be wise for you to seek more information about anorexia and bulimia and also to contact a counselor or physician to determine what kind of assistance would be most helpful for you. Anorexia nervosa and bulimia can be overcome with the proper support and counsel. The earlier you seek help, the better, although it is never too late to start on the road to recovery.

In this first chapter, I introduced you to several people struggling with anorexia and bulimia. You have been informed of current facts and statistics concerning the eating disorder epidemic and have had a chance to evaluate your tendencies toward anorexia and bulimia. It is my prayer that this chapter has given you some insight and that chapter 2 will help you continue to gain personal insights and increased self-awareness about factors that contribute to anorexic and bulimic behavior.

CHAPTER 1, NOTES

1. Steven Levenkron, quoted in Fran Arman, "Anorexia Nervosa," *The Psych Review*, a publication of the Brea Hospital Neuropsychiatric Center, 875 N. Brea Blvd., Brea, CA 92621.

2. Ibid.

3. Steven Levenkron, quoted in A. A. Lucas, J. W. Duncan, and V. Piens, "The Treatment of Anorexia Nervosa," *American Journal of Psychiatry* 133 (1976):1034-1038.

4. Eating disorders seminar by K. Kim Lampson, Providence Medical Center, Seattle, Washington, May 13-14, 1983.

5. Dr. Myron Winick, "Nutrition in American Women," *Columbia University Journal of Nutrition and Health*, p. 2.

6. Lampson seminar.

7. H. Pope and J. Hudson, seminar on bulimia; and their book, *New Hope for Binge Eaters* (New York: Harper and Row, 1984).

8. Raymond Vath, eating disorder symposium at Cedar Hills Hospital, Portland, Oregon, 7 October 1983.

9. J. Allan Ryan, "Weight Reduction in Wrestling," *The Physician and Sports Medicine* 9 (September 1981):78-93.

10. Eric Levin, "A Lethal Guest for the Winning Edge," *People Magazine*, 22 August 1983, p. 22.

11. Marlene Boskind-White and William C. White, *Bulimarexia: The Binge-Purge Cycle* (New York: W. W. Norton and Co., 1983), p.45.

2

BEGINNING
THE PROCESS OF
SELF-AWARENESS

Ever since she was a baby, Linda had been fat. Her parents used to call her their "little teddy bear" because she was so cuddly and pudgy. She showed me a photo from her childhood scrapbook, one she swears to someday burn. In the picture she is grinning from ear to ear. Her arms are puffed out of a sleeveless shirt that is partially buttoned over a pregnant-looking tummy. She hates that picture and all the memories that were attached to being known as a "fat kid."

Months before I met her, Linda tried out for cheerleader. All of her close friends told her she was the most skilled of all those competing. When the big day of tryouts came, she performed perfectly. Everyone, including Linda, thought she would be selected. The next morning she left for school, excited as she anticipated seeing her name on the list of the new rally squad members.

Then came the shocking truth. Her name wasn't on the list. She couldn't believe it. What had gone wrong? She knew she had done better than the other girls at tryouts. Why wasn't her name posted?

She ran down the hall to find the cheerleading advisor—maybe she could give her some answers. Mrs. Anderson stood up as Linda walked into her office in tears. "Why didn't I make the squad when everyone, including you, said I was so good?" Linda cried. Mrs. Anderson's reply made a scarring impression on Linda. She said, "You're good, but you're also overweight. We can't put fat cheerleaders out in front of everyone. Besides that, we don't have a uniform big enough to fit you."

Stunned, Linda slowly walked out of Mrs. Anderson's office. She hated herself. She hated her fat. She determined at that moment never to put another fattening food in her mouth. During the weeks that followed, she lived on water, lettuce, and celery.

Two months later, Linda had lost forty pounds

and had gone from a size thirteen to a size four. At 5'7", she weighed 102 lbs. Linda had become a victim of anorexia nervosa at fifteen years of age.

I began to meet with Linda shortly after her confrontation with Mrs. Anderson. I sensed her tremendous inner fear of "getting fat." When she looked in the mirror at her emaciated body, the reflection she saw was the image from the scrapbook photograph. When others expressed concern about her frail, weak appearance, she was convinced they were trying to control her and wanted her to be fat. She felt like everyone was on one side of a line, ganged up against her, while she stood on the other side—alone.

Linda sincerely believed that her acceptance by others hinged on keeping her weight at 102 pounds. Even a one pound gain could mean rejection by others. Since her weight loss, boys were suddenly flocking around her. She loved the attention and the dates, but was paranoid that all interest would be lost if she ate normally.

Linda is now sixteen and making good progress in fighting against self-starvation. But the road to healing has been one of dedication and commitment on her part. She has worked hard to understand herself and those things which contribute to her anorexic behavior.

YOUR PERSONAL MISSION: INCREASED SELF-AWARENESS

It is my conviction that Satan, the Christian's archenemy, would like nothing more than to keep you ignorant and feeling helpless. If he can keep you from understanding how to escape from your prison, his mission will have been accomplished. John 10:10 says, "the thief [Satan] comes only to steal and kill and destroy." He wants to keep you duped. That verse goes on to say that Jesus has come to give you life—abundant life. God's desire is for you to walk in the light of understanding and self-awareness. As you become more in tune with who you are as one of God's most prized creations, you will be in a better position to move toward healing and wholeness.

I have found in counseling that everyone has unique beliefs about weight and eating behaviors. When Linda gained insights about her behavior, she began to be healed. I'd like to help you understand your eating disorder. This is the first step to unlocking the door of your prison.

Before you proceed to the next chapter, I greatly encourage you to take the time to carefully and honestly work through the following exercises. They will lead you to specific insights about yourself. Sometimes looking inside yourself is not a comfortable adventure. It's never fun rummaging through dirty laundry, but before the clothes can be cleaned, the items need to be organized into piles. These questions can help you sort through some of your thoughts and feelings. It may be painful, but it is in no way harmful. In fact, it will be healthful.

Before you begin, pray this prayer.

> Dear God . . . I thank You that You love me. I thank You that You are intimately acquainted with every aspect of my life. You love me unconditionally and want to help me heal. As I begin this mission of self-awareness, please give me insight and understanding. Bring into my mind those things that will most help me understand my eating disorder. Give me courage. Give me strength. Be with me in a special way as I complete these questions. Thank you, God.

1. When did you first get involved in anorexia nervosa or bulimia?

2. What were the situations or circumstances that surrounded the onset of your anorexia nervosa or bulimia?

3. How did you ever come up with the idea to starve or binge and purge? Did any other person play a part in giving you the idea?

4. What feelings did you have when you answered questions 1-3? List as many as you can.

5. How long have you been involved in starving or bingeing and purging?

6. Have there ever been times when you stopped starving or bingeing and purging? When? What were the circumstances during that time in your life?

7. What reasons do you have for wanting to starve or binge and purge? (List at least eight reasons—dig deep.)

8. Do your friends starve or binge and purge? How many of them? How close are they to you?

9. What feelings did you have while answering questions 5-8?

10. I want you to picture yourself planning a full-blown binge. What is it that you look forward to?

11. Now, picture yourself not eating for an entire day. What are the benefits or payoffs for making it all day without eating?

12. When is it easiest for you to binge or starve? In what situations?

COMMON EXCUSES FOR BINGEING AND PURGING AND/OR STARVING

When the above questions are asked in my support and growth groups, I get an assortment of answers. If you had some difficulty pinpointing some of the reasons you binge or starve or the rationale you use, you might like to look at what others have noted. As you do, it will become apparent that you are not alone; others feel and think in ways similar to you.

41

You'll see this verse come alive: "But remember this—the wrong desires that come into your life aren't anything new and different. Many others have faced exactly the same problems before you. . . . You can trust God to keep the temptation from becoming so strong that you can't stand up against it, for he has promised this and will do what he says" (1 Corinthians 10:13 TLB).

As you read, note how these statements reflect your own attitudes and reasoning.

EXCUSES FOR BINGEING AND PURGING

Food acts as my friend. "When I'm lonely and have no one else to be with, I can always submerge myself in ice cream and cookies."

"Every night I have a big bowl of ice cream while I sit in bed under a warm electric blanket with three or four pillows propped up behind me. I usually eat slowly and read a good book at the same time. If anyone interrupts me or the phone rings or I'm deprived of my ice cream in bed, I feel angry and cheated. It's my special food, at my special time, in my special place—that brings real satisfaction."

Food reduces my anxiety and frustration. "When I come home after a hectic day working for my boss, I find peace in fixing gourmet dishes and eating every last bite. Food won't argue with me, put me down, or turn on me. It only brings instant gratification and pleasure."

"The pressures of life overwhelm me sometimes so that all I want to do is find an escape from my constant worries. I can ignore the worries if I stuff them down with a box of Twinkies or cupcakes."

Food entertains me. "It's no fun to watch TV without popcorn, sandwiches, chips, or something to eat. And when my favorite shows come on the air, that's the best time for dessert—I get a double whammy of entertainment that way."

If I don't eat it, someone else will. "Mom made cherry pie over the holidays. There were three pieces left in the pan and I ate them all in one sitting. I figured if I didn't eat them right away, someone else would get to them, and I'd miss out completely."

It was their fault. "I binged because they set me off. They offered me a piece of cake while I was baby-sitting, and I ate the whole thing after they left. When they got home, I told them the cat knocked it on the floor so I put it down the garbage disposal. It was their own fault for setting me off like that."

"When I was growing up, Mom and Dad always told me about the starving children in India. When I look at food on my plate, I feel I must eat every bite. If I don't, I feel guilty. But then after I eat all the food I feel guilty for feeling so full. Then I want to binge and vomit so I can get rid of the guilt."

I deserve to binge. "I've gone all day without food. The diet Pepsi and coffee kept me going, and since I was successful all day, I deserve to binge. I owe it to myself."

I already blew it, so why fight it? "I've been on a rigid diet lately that allows only certain prescribed foods. My friend baked some fresh chocolate chip cookies, and I ate two of them before leaving her house. On the way home I figured, 'Oh well, I've blown my diet already, I might as well really do it good.' So I stopped at a grocery store, spent $10.00 on candy and junk food, and went on an all-out binge."

There's a financial payoff, so why not enjoy all I can? "Since my friend is paying the bill today, I should choose a big item on the menu. After all, I don't get taken out to dinner very often."

"Candy bars on sale, six for a dollar, a savings of fifty cents. I can't pass up a deal like that. It's a virtuous quality to hunt and find bargain deals."

I want to keep people happy during the holidays. "The holidays are perfect setups for a binge. Everyone fixes all my favorite foods. Why fight it? It's easier just to eat it all and then vomit. That keeps the cook happy and me skinny."

43

EXCUSES FOR STARVING

Food is my source of power. "I'm in charge of this area of my life. No one can make me eat. The harder others try to make me eat, the more powerful I feel because I can win."

Today I have to starve. "I ate too much yesterday. I have to starve myself today or I'll end up looking like a blimp."

My rituals are important to me. "I have a set routine that I stick to every day. Coffee at 7:30 A.M., an orange at noon, and celery and carrots at 6:00 P.M. It really feels good to be able to set my eating goals each morning and then to go to bed at night knowing I've accomplished those goals."

I deserve to be punished. "I binged so badly last night that I have to run twenty miles today and skip meals. It was terrible of me to behave in such a childish way. I need to beat my body for performing so poorly."

They deserve to be punished. "They haven't been fair to me lately. They look at me like I'm not important and like they don't care. If they want to treat me like that, then fine. I can play the game, too—I won't eat. That will show them I don't care how they treat me, and punish them for being so mean to me."

I like to show that I'm in control. "I can beat those hunger pains. When my stomach starts to growl, I just ignore it. I figure if I ignore the pangs long enough, they'll just go away. Sometimes I can trick the growls with a diet coke and then they quiet down."

"I find great satisfaction in seeing others eat. One of my favorite pastimes is to fix beautiful gourmet dishes for my family. Of course, I wouldn't think of indulging in all those fattening calories with them. I'm stronger than that."

My desire is that these last few pages have helped you become aware of some of the common excuses that are involved with starving and bingeing. Eating disorders do not happen in a vacuum. It is important to realize that there are underlying factors and surrounding events that contribute to any eating disorder. Once you become aware of what motivates you to starve or binge and purge or both, you are in a position to do something about it.

In this chapter we have looked at some general excuses that are frequently expressed by those with eating disorders. In the next chapter, we'll look at some of the more specific irrational beliefs that keep people locked into starving and bingeing. You'll not only learn some effective ways to challenge irrational ideas, you will learn some ways to build a healthy perspective. The goal is to help you discover some of the barriers that may be keeping you from making progress in your healing, and then to give you some tools that will help you win your personal battle.

IRRATIONAL BELIEFS: BARRIERS TO CHANGE

A twenty-two-year-old woman who had formerly been a national winner in the 100-yard dash sat across from me. Her shapely figure and well-toned muscles were the envy of all of her friends. Everyone viewed Patty as a winner—except Patty. Because she had bulimia, Patty had lost sight of the truth that she was a worthwhile person. All she sensed when she ran her daily ten miles was that she was a failure—a woman whipped by food.

During a counseling session one afternoon, she put her hands on her hips, tightened her lips, and said, "It's just too hard to change. Whenever I try not to binge and vomit, I get more uptight than when I give in. I move into a panic mode and feel totally out of control. It's similar to what I've heard heroin addicts go through during cold turkey withdrawal. I get shaky, edgy, and feel as if I'm on the brink of losing my sanity. I'd rather just forget about being self-controlled and not work at it. At least that way I wouldn't have to spend so much energy fighting my desire to eat. If I could just give in and accept this disorder as part of my life, I could put my energy into other things."

I had heard rationalizations like that before, so I concentrated on helping Patty explore the ideas she had just communicated. It became apparent to Patty that she was defending her behavior. We talked about why it was irrational for her to think that fighting her eating disorder was a waste of energy. I said, "Patty, I would be less than a good therapist if I let you walk out the door today without challenging your rationalizations."

After a few tears and several wadded tissues, Patty decided that she wanted to fight to win the battle against her bulimia. With a trembling voice, she muttered, "I guess I really wouldn't save any energy by giving up. Besides, what good will left over energy do me if I'm dead? It looks like the only way to beat my bulimia is to face it, and take it one step at a time."

THE DANGER OF IRRATIONAL THINKING

You may have had thoughts similar to Patty's. Your barriers to change may be packaged differently, but all of us use defenses to protect ourselves from looking at the "unacceptable" parts of our lives. However, rationalizing a destructive behavior can be very dangerous, especially when it becomes a lifestyle.

Let me illustrate what I'm saying. Picture yourself holding a champagne glass full of a red, liquid rat killer. It looks absolutely beautiful, the aroma is enticing, and you have been told that it tastes delicious. In your mind you think, "This stuff looks too delicious to be able to hurt me." So you decide to drink it. The result? You are dead in two minutes. Now, everything you observed about the drink was true . . . it was beautiful, aromatic, and tasted great. On the outside it looked appealing, and drinking it seemed to make sense. However, there was one problem. You denied it was poison.

You based your decision to drink on the irrational belief that the rat poison wouldn't hurt you. The result . . . death. Many people with anorexia nervosa and bulimia justify their behavior with irrational beliefs. Some even say, "This eating disorder is such a good form of weight control, it could never hurt me." But eating disorders can and do at times result in fatalities.

BEGIN TO CHALLENGE YOUR IRRATIONAL BELIEFS

Let me encourage you to get in touch with your irrational beliefs. I want to see you come to wholeness. And deep down, you want to see yourself freed from your obsession. Take the next few minutes to discover some of your barricades to change. Then together we'll try to knock down and break apart those obstructions.

A lot of your progress will be determined by the thoughts that habitually occupy your mind. If you constantly think self-defeating, irrational beliefs, you'll be defeated by your disorder. However, if you *practice* (I say

49

practice because this does take work) thinking thoughts that counteract those irrational ideas, you will develop a strong sense that you are competent to handle your eating problem.

Research and experience have proven that a habit of challenging irrational beliefs builds confidence and strength when those beliefs are replaced with rational truths. The irrational beliefs you use today sank their roots into your lifestyle in the past. Now is your chance to begin to weed out those destructive roots one by one. Let's demolish some of those irrational personal lies. Below I've listed some of the irrational beliefs that are frequently voiced by eating-disorder victims. Do you see yourself between the lines?

IDENTIFYING IRRATIONAL BELIEFS ABOUT YOUR BEHAVIOR

Irrational belief #1. "I don't want to try to quit this behavior because I know it will just happen again."

Will it? You are assuming the worst. I know many recovered anorexics and bulimics who would strongly disagree with this statement. Remind yourself of the truth, "I can do all things through Him who strengthens me" (Philippians 4:13 NASB). If you depend on God's help, every step you take in the direction of healing will be empowered by Him.

You can set yourself up for failure by believing you will fail. Try something new. Instead of focusing on failure, why not focus on this idea: "If I get help, there's a good chance I will recover and that my eating disorder won't paralyze me for the rest of my life." See yourself getting help and being successful; your behavior will follow suit. Say, "I do want to quit because there are no guarantees that my eating disorder will suddenly come back once I'm well. I have good cause to think that if others can do it, there's hope for me. Nothing is impossible with God's help."

Others, like Patty, state their belief in the inevitability of failure differently. "It's too hard to change. I'll waste too much energy trying and end up losing in the end. So—why bother?"

You're right. It does take energy to change. But it takes *more energy* to live with yourself in a defeated state. Anorexia and bulimia steal time and drain energy out of their victims.

On the other hand, a determination and drive to overcome an eating disorder can actually sponsor internal power and energy. I remember meeting with Linda after she had accomplished one of the goals made during our previous session together. She had decided not to go to the third floor of her office building for one week. (This was where the candy and pop machines were located and where Linda usually spent five dollars a day on an afternoon binge.) She bounced into my office with a smile from ear to ear and said, "I did it! I didn't go to the third floor all week. I actually cut my number of binges in half!" Just one week before, she had been lethargic and apathetic. Her choice to exercise self-control gave her energy and enthusiasm.

I've also heard this irrational belief modified to, "If I try hard today and eat normally, and then fail tomorrow, I'll feel even worse than if I had never tried." In other words, success today will make tomorrow's defeat even more unbearable. This may seem logical, but the statement lacks a long-term perspective. It is considering only today and tomorrow, not the overall picture.

This short-term perspective doesn't acknowledge that the person who does not binge and purge today but does tomorrow is still better off than if she had binged and purged both days. The anorexic who eats 500 calories today and 0 calories tomorrow is still 500 calories successfully ahead of her previous pattern of eating 0 calories for twenty days.

It is important to view success and failure from a long-term perspective. Try saying, "I'll eat normally today, and if I fail tomorrow, well, I'm sure it will be a disappointment, but at least I'm a few steps ahead of myself by tackling today successfully."

Irrational Belief #2. "The best way to stay thin is the way I'm doing it now."

One of the easiest ways to challenge this rationalization is simply to say, "That's a lie! My eating disorder is not the only means I can use to stay thin." Think of the slender people you know. Do all of them have an eating disorder? It helps to consider that there are a lot of thin people in the world who know absolutely nothing about starving, bingeing, or purging.

Your way of staying thin is *one* way. It is also a life-threatening way. There are many alternatives in weight control that are successful and healthy. Don't be duped by the lie that says, "My way is the only way."

Let's practice challenging that irrational statement. Say out loud, "Starving (and/or bingeing and purging) is not the only way to thinness. It is one of the best ways, though, to destroy my organs, deplete my energy, and ruin my life. Looking for healthy weight control alternatives is one of the smartest moves I could make at this time in my life." Read it again, and let these healthy statements begin to sink into the recesses of your mind.

Irrational Belief #3. "This eating behavior is my life. If I give it up, I will have nothing to do."

Perhaps your eating disorder began out of boredom. Valerie said, "When I lost my job, I had nothing to do. So—I ate. I ate all day long and then took laxatives to push the food through my system."

Although eating is a way to reduce boredom, it certainly is not the most fulfilling way, especially when done to an extreme. Valerie will be the first to tell you that food is a false substitute for fulfillment. Her despair and guilt for her behavior far outweighed any satisfaction she felt.

What are some things you've always wanted to do? Are there some hobbies or interests that you could cultivate? Have you thought about the possibility of building up some old friendships and starting some new ones? What kind of community activities are convenient and available to you?

In the chapters ahead, we will consider some options for diversions from eating. For now, refute your irrational belief by saying, "As I recover, I'll have more time to do things I've always wanted to do. As I take steps toward facing myself and my problem, I will win more victories. My success will build my strength and confidence, and it will become easier for me to get involved with people and activities. It may mean that I'll have to take some risks, but my life will actually be more enriched, and I won't be bored."

Irrational Belief #4. "My favorite escape from my problems is food. If I give up this area of my life, I'll have to deal with all those other sore spots, and I don't want to."

It is true that as the overpowering problem of bulimia or anorexia diminishes, an individual may become more aware of other parts of life that need attention and repair. But this is nothing to dread.

Be encouraged. In the process of overcoming an eating disorder, you will collect tools that can be used in other problem areas of your life. These tools will help you cope with a variety of stresses. You will build a track record of victories. As you use these tools, you will gradually become more skillful at handling any new challenges.

You may not want to deal with your problems because you fear you'll fail. You picture problems tackling you rather than you tackling problems. You need not fear. Growth is a process. God is at work in you. "Fight the good fight of the faith" (1 Timothy 6:12). You'll be more competent and qualified to cope with life's pressures if you are actively fighting against your eating disorder.

A favorite verse that I use to tear down fear barriers in my own life is 2 Timothy 1:7, "For God hath not given us a spirit of fear, but of power, and of love, and of a sound mind" (KJV). If you are afraid and find yourself ruminating on fearful thoughts, speak this verse out loud. It will squeeze out those self-defeating ideas and replace them with victory truths. It helps me to talk to God while using this verse. I might say something like, "God, I thank You that You have not given me a spirit of fear. Instead You have given me a spirit of power, and love, and a sound mind. God, I refuse to believe those fearful thoughts. Instead, I choose to believe You are my God, and that You are with me constantly, helping me toward healing. Anything else is a lie."

I need to add here that many people think that once their eating disorder is cured, the rest of life will be total bliss. This is a misconception. You might have said to yourself, "If I could just get out of this bondage to food, my life would be free from problems." Don't delude yourself. No one lives problem free. Problems are a natural part of human experience. But with God, all problems can be faced. In fact, many times those problems provide platforms from which we can watch God do the miraculous.

Irrational Belief #5. "I'm happy with my life the way it is." Are you really being honest? Picture yourself in your favorite bathroom purging the food from your last binge. Are you happy? Picture yourself taking all those laxatives and the cramping and pain that follows. Are you happy with yourself?

Denial can be deadly. I'm sure there are parts of your life that you thoroughly enjoy. I rejoice with you! However, those points of happiness will become progressively less enjoyable the longer you deny an eating disorder problem.

When you find yourself saying, "I'm happy with my life the way it is," dispute that personal lie with: "Who am I kidding? I don't enjoy the emotional pain and bondage I feel. I hate it. So there's no use lying to myself. It's time to get started with a new life. It's time for new beginnings. It's time to work toward really living and forget about merely existing. After all, I'm worth it!"

IRRATIONAL BELIEFS ABOUT MY BEHAVIOR IN RELATION TO OTHERS

Irrational Belief #6. "My eating disorder is the one thing I can use to show other people that I am in control."

But you are not in control when you're in bondage to an eating disorder. You are out of control. Control was lost when you began to fight for gasps of air while drowning in the waves of your disorder.

Often the families of those with eating disorders are very close and overly dependent on one another. Sometimes this results in the eating disorder victim's being treated as a dependent child rather than as an autonomous, capable individual. I've heard many bulimics and anorexics say, "People treat me like a kid and like I don't have a mind of my own. Food is the one area of my life that they can't touch."

People may act as if you don't have a mind of your own, but you can prove them wrong. How? By taking charge of this area of your life and successfully recovering. The only person who will really lose if the eating disorder continues is you. If you think that others are against you, do you want to give them the satisfaction of seeing you progressively get worse? As you work with God toward healing, others will be forced to stand back and notice your success.

Try challenging this lie with ideas like these: "I'm going to prove to myself and others that I can conquer this eating disorder. People may treat me as though I don't have a mind of my own, but they'll have to change their opinion when they see my new lifestyle. The more control I take to get well, the less people will try to control me. At this point, getting well is really worth the reward of getting others off my back."

Irrational Belief #7. "I have to continue this pattern because my friends won't care about me if I'm well and don't have this problem anymore."

Sometimes being sick does have payoffs. You get a lot of attention and tender loving care from friends. Chances are you have had extra attention since you developed your eating disorder. That's fine for right now. But I must warn you that ninety-nine percent of the time people get bored, tired, and exasperated with someone who doesn't take responsibility for problems that can be remedied.

Everyone has problems. Some are more difficult to cope with than others. Your friends have their own struggles. They are having to take responsibility for them. If every time they are with you, they find themselves drained and frustrated because of your irresponsible behavior, they might not stick around very long.

Consider the people you know. Are you drawn to individuals who have positive insights during the ups and downs of life and who take responsibility for their actions? Or are you drawn to those who constantly blame others for their unhappiness and expect people to cater to their needs? What kind of person do you want to be? Life is so much more rewarding when it is lived to the fullest.

You might like to practice combating this personal lie with statements like these: "My friends will enjoy me more when they know I'm taking charge of this area of my life. They'll respect me for taking responsibility to get help. I'll enjoy my friends more, too. I don't want them to feel sorry for me anymore or to give me attention for being sick. I want to take steps to recover so that they can spend time with me because they like me, not because they are worried about me."

Irrational Belief #8. "I don't want to deal with sensual advances from the opposite sex. If I give up my eating disorder, I may become more appealing, and I'm not sure I could handle a come-on. This way I can avoid my sexuality."

This is another rationalization that is built on fear. Think about it. What proof is there that someone won't make an advance toward you today? None. There is as good a chance that you'll receive a "come-on" today as there is that you'll receive one tomorrow or next week. Let's consider what you could do about this should the situation arise.

Having a battle plan is helpful. I have a few statements I keep on the back burner just in case someone tries to get "fresh" with me. For example, if a man were to try to ask me out for a date, I might kindly reply with, "Only if I can bring my husband along," or "I'm happily married and really not interested." If you are single and not interested in someone who is making advances toward you, remember that honesty is often best. Politely tell the person, "I'm not interested!" It's amazing to see the profound impact those three little words can have.

If you are fighting your eating disorder, gaining tools, and growing personally, you'll be in a much better position to handle a sexual advance than if you are in the pits of defeat. Feeling like a failure can make you vulnerable. But feeling like you're making progress can leave you with spunk to deal creatively with those potential advances.

Irrational Belief #9. "My family is so preoccupied with the way I eat that if I start eating again, they'll be on my back about everything I put in my mouth."

Sometimes family members can be so concerned about the person with an eating disorder that they act like detectives and watch every move made toward the kitchen or every bite eaten during meals. When this happens you naturally feel your privacy has been invaded.

Let me add some perspective to your feelings of intrusion. If your family or friends didn't care about you, they wouldn't give your behavior a second thought. If you are feeling watched over, it's because those who love you want to help you. *They just don't know how to offer assistance.* They may think the only help they can give is to make you stop eating certain foods if you have been bingeing or to make you eat if you have been starving.

I know. It doesn't work. But realize that their intentions are good. The bottom line is that only you can take responsibility for your problem. You must seek help and deal with your eating disorder. No one can do it for you.

This is why family therapy is so important for those with eating disorders. It is vital to your progress that those you live with and who are closest to you learn how they can help you. Right now, they may be constantly "on your back," not realizing what they are doing. A professional counselor can help alleviate this problem by talking with your family about how they can encourage you.

I have seen tremendous healing occur in families when they received insight concerning what does and doesn't help a recovering anorexic or bulimic. After you have had a chance to talk confidentially with a counselor, your recovery speed can be boosted if you take the risk of involving loved ones in therapy. You might get a chance to watch the Sherlock Holmes in your family phase into retirement. (Chapter 13 can give your loved ones some helpful hints about ways they can support you as you work toward wholeness.)

Irrational Belief #10. "I can use my eating disorder as a scapegoat now. If people reject me, I can say it's because I'm anorexic or bulimic. If I give up this eating disorder, I'll have nothing safe on which to blame rejection."

We all look for scapegoats. It seems so much easier to shift responsibility than to deal constructively with problems. However, as we gloss over rejections by saying, "It's because I'm fat, or bulimic, or anorexic," we also pass up opportunities to learn about ourselves and our relationships with others. Chances are your eating disorder may have nothing to do with the reasons others keep their distance from you. Maybe people feel you don't like them or that you aren't interested in their lives. Maybe they don't realize your desire to make friends.

Davia was always feeling rejected. When she went to church, she usually sat by herself. She said, "Whenever I go to any of the college functions, people don't talk to me. They stay in their own little circles." I asked Davia if she had ever taken the risk of approaching one or two people in the group on her own initiative. Her reply was, "Oh no! I couldn't do that. The others have their own groups of friends and don't need anyone else to barge in on their relationships."

For the next few minutes Davia and I talked about the fact that regardless of outward appearances, all of us are a little bit insecure and fearful at times. We tried to gain a more realistic perspective about the college group functions. Part of this perspective included the idea that every person coming didn't "have it all together," and that most likely there were many others who felt just as uncertain and insecure as she did.

Davia set a goal that week to go to the college group and to find one person who was alone. Once she found someone, she would share her name, a little information about her school and work, and then ask the other person some general questions to show that she was interested in getting to know them.

The following week Davia came back with a sparkle in her eyes. She had made a new friend. She discovered that as she was friendly and showed interest and care, the friendliness was returned. Instead of saying, "I might be rejected," and pinning the blame on her bulimia, she said, "I'll take the risk of showing I'm interested."

It is so much healthier not to hang on to scapegoats. As you let go of them, you'll learn more about yourself and the way you relate to others. In the process of making new friends, we all experience the sting of rejection at one time or another. Sometimes there are not even any good reasons for the rejection. Now, that hurts. But with God's strength you can handle it. There is no need to let one person's rejection destroy the rest of your life.

Instead of using your bulimia or anorexia as a scapegoat, try this rationale for coping with rejection: "I may be rejected as I take the risk of making friends, but I can handle it because God has said He will never leave me or forsake me. If I get rejected, I can talk to God about my hurt and ask Him to heal the wound. But chances are I'll make more friends than I thought possible because there are a lot of people in the world who need to be needed. I'm going to find someone this week I can show interest in and encourage. Maybe other people won't make my week, but I can certainly try to encourage someone else by reaching out."

Think of someone you know who may need a friendly boost by a kind word. If no one comes to mind, pray and ask God to bring someone across your path this week whom you can encourage. Then watch God bless.

This chapter has discussed only ten specific irrational beliefs that frequently keep the eating disorder victim imprisoned. You may be aware of other ideas you have believed which have blocked you from moving toward wholeness. Use these insights and begin to challenge destructive and irrational thoughts. Be honest with yourself. As you are, God will honor your efforts and back you up one hundred percent. When everything seems to be crumbling down around you and you feel like a hopeless case, remember you and God as a team are a majority!

PART 2

PIECES
OF THE
PUZZLE

YOU ARE
PRICELESS!

I'd like you to meet Patsy and Rachel. On the outside they look like they have it all together. But on the inside they're falling apart. As with many eating disorder victims, their self-esteem has been crushed in their attempts to establish their value and worth on society's standards. You'll sense their despair as you read their scenarios.

"I might as well eat. I'm not good at anything else," Patsy thought as she stormed in after school. The day had been a disaster—she had received a *C* on her chemistry exam and had been ridiculed in speech class by her teacher. Thinking she would gain some comfort from food, she headed for the refrigerator. Patsy swallowed her frustrations with a gallon of peppermint ice cream and a bottle of chocolate sauce. An hour later she hated herself for gorging. As she flopped down on the couch in misery, her father's words pierced her thoughts, "You'll never amount to anything!" Patsy was convinced her father was right . . . she was a loser.

Rachel, a thirty-three-year-old businesswoman, used self-starvation methods to keep her size five figure. She took great pride in having the smallest and best dressed body at the office. For eight years she struggled through a doctoral program in business. Three years later, when she was operating as her company's top sales manager, the axe fell. The depressed economy had driven the chairman of the board to lay off forty percent of his employees. Her entire department was cut. Disillusioned with the corporate system and frustrated by her inability to quit starving, Rachel felt worthless.

Rachel and Patsy's self-hatred is typical of individuals with eating disorders. They *expect* excellence from themselves and are seldom satisfied despite their achievements. For them, overachievement and perfection are the norm rather than the exception. Although new heights of expertise are reached, they feel their performance is average or mediocre. The constant tension of striving to be a superwoman or a superman takes its toll on their self-esteem when the impossible goal of being perfect is never achieved.

You'll be encouraged to hear that Patsy and Rachael no longer have shattered self-esteem. They no longer see themselves as losers. As they chose to deal with their eating disorder, they were able to crawl out of that pit of self-hate and catch a glimpse of their real beauty. I'd like to tell you some of the healing agents that helped them repair their bruised and broken self-images. Their starting point was learning the difference between self-esteem, self-pride, and self-hate.

UNDERSTANDING SELF-ESTEEM

We hear the catch-all term *self-esteem* used often. What exactly does it imply? Put simply, self-esteem is the appreciation one has for his or her own value and worth.

Many Christians confuse the sin of pride with the godly characteristic of loving yourself in a healthy way. Rachel and Patsy struggled with this confusion. It helped them to see the difference between self-esteem, self-pride, and self-hate drawn in picture form, like the diagram below.

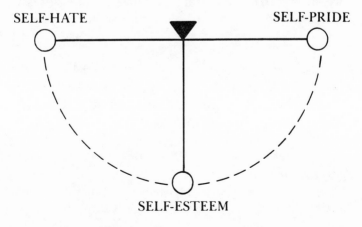

SELF-HATE   SELF-PRIDE

SELF-ESTEEM

We can think of these three concepts while picturing a pendulum. When the pendulum swings to the extreme right, it stops at self-pride. Here a person exaggerates his own value to a warped extreme. He has tunnel vision and actually believes he can do no wrong. He doesn't need God. He doesn't need people. His motto in life is "the most important thing in life is me. Step aside, I'm coming through."

When the pendulum swings to the far left, it stops at self-hate. Here a person degrades himself to a warped extreme. Like the person with self-pride, he has tunnel vision. He believes he can do nothing right. He's convinced that God doesn't want him and that people don't like him. In his despair, he often wonders why he was even born.

As you can see in the diagram, self-hate and self-pride are opposite extremes. Both are severely out of balance and counterproductive. Living a life of either self-hate or self-pride is crippling. A balance must be reached.

Self-esteem is the healthy balance in the middle. The person with self-esteem understands that he has intrinsic value. He realizes his need for God and others. He has a clear perspective of both his strengths and weaknesses. He isn't afraid to square his shoulders and joyfully declare, "Since God loves me, I can love myself!"

Most eating disorder victims tend to swing to the far left of the picture, toward self-hate, because they're involved in the destructive pattern of evaluating their worth and value on the basis of appearance and performance. They don't realize that this is a set-up for despair.

There is no such thing as a perfect body, a perfect intellect—a perfect anything this side of heaven. When value is gauged by the ability to be perfect, rest assured failure and defeat are lurking in the wings.

Through our times together, Patsy and Rachel gradually came to believe that it was good for them to love themselves. Smiles returned to their faces as they rebuilt their shattered self-esteem. As they began to understand the difference between self-pride, self-esteem, and self-hate, they set out on a mission to build their self-esteem on a solid basis rather than on society's standards. The rest of this chapter covers some of the insights they learned in the building process.

BUILDING SELF-ESTEEM ON A SOLID FOUNDATION

KNOW WHO YOU ARE

We are often experts at scrutinizing ourselves and knowing who we are not. This limited perspective is depressing—and it blinds us from seeing who we really are! Romans 12:3 says, "Rightly evaluate yourselves; evaluate yourselves with a wise judgment" (Phillips). In other words, get in touch with who you are. I want to help you begin to celebrate you.

For the celebration to begin, you'll need to uncover some of the things that are unique to you. Take a couple of minutes and describe yourself. Put down as many things as come to mind (e.g., joyful, fun-loving, detail-oriented). What are your strengths? What do you like about yourself? Force yourself to recognize your good points; this is a crucial step toward building self-esteem.

Why did God make you as He did? So that you could be like everyone else? No! He fashioned you in a special way because He wanted you to make a unique statement and to leave a unique impression on the world you touch. There is no one—and will never be anyone—who is your exact equal. You are an original. You're not a mass-marketed copy hot off an assembly line. God, the Master of all creativity, has made you different from everyone else. Embrace who you are and celebrate your uniqueness.

69

Psalm 139 tells us that from the moment of conception, God was involved in creating a masterpiece. You and I are wonderfully made.

"For you created my inmost being; you knit me together in my mother's womb. I praise you because I am fearfully and wonderfully made; your works are wonderful, I know that full well. My frame was not hidden from you when I was made in the secret place. When I was woven together in the depths of the earth, your eyes saw my unformed body. All the days ordained for me were written in your book before one of them came to be" (Psalm 139:13-16).

RECOGNIZE THAT GOD LOVES YOU

Jane had been anorexic for six years and bulimic for three. She felt like she had made a total mess of her life and that God wanted nothing to do with her. She was certain that He had turned His back on her long ago.

One afternoon she cried, "God doesn't care about me. If I were worth anything at all to God, He would not have given me the parents I had. My dad was always gone on business trips and my mom was an alcoholic. I had a rotten childhood. I remember nights when I cried myself to sleep, begging God to help me. He never answered. I always figured I wasn't good enough to deserve His answer. Maybe if I had been a better daughter, Dad would have stayed home and Mom would have stopped drinking. Maybe if I had stopped vomiting God would have listened." Jane could not believe God loved her or that she should love herself.

We looked in the Bible together to find some answers for Jane's questions about her value to God. Our search led to the discovery of some amazing truths that helped her understand God and rebuild her low self-esteem. Let these truths be an encouragement to you, too.

When you are at your worst, God loves you. Romans 5:8 says, "But God demonstrates his own love for us in this: While we were still sinners, Christ died for us." You don't have to clean up your act to ask God for help. He loves you so much that even while knowing about your failures and sins, He died for you. He loves you in spite of what you have done—or not done—in spite of your eating disorder.

God wants to have an intimate relationship with you—even when you feel defeated. In Matthew 11 Jesus speaks these words to those who are bruised, bleeding, or broken: "Come to me, all you who are weary and burdened, and I will give you rest. Take my yoke upon you and learn from me, for I am gentle and humble in heart, and you will find rest for your souls. For my yoke is easy and my burden is light" (vv. 28-30).

Jesus wants so much to have a close relationship with you. You don't have to be perfect to open the door of your heart to Him. Once you have opened your heart to Christ and have acknowledged your need of a Savior, He will begin a relationship with you to which nothing in this life can compare. He does not promise to take away your disorder, but He will help you as you take steps toward wholeness and health. Jesus didn't come to help those who were perfect. He came to die for imperfect humans like you and me with all our frailties. Yes, even people with eating disorders. You can trust Him to help you as you draw near to Him (James 4:8).

God is not out to punish and condemn you. So many I talk with are convinced that God is punishing them by giving them an eating disorder. This is a misunderstanding of how God relates to us.

If you have trusted in Jesus Christ, He has forgiven all your sins and failures. All of them, not just some of them. Colossians 2:13-14 says, "[God] forgave us *all* our sins, having canceled the written code, with its regulations, that was against us and that stood opposed

71

to us; he took it away, nailing it to the cross" (italics mine). God is not punishing you by giving you anorexia or bulimia. You may be punishing yourself and affirming your own self-hatred, but God loves you.

You are a source of great pleasure to God. Psalm 149:4 says, "For the LORD takes delight in his people." God finds great pleasure in His children and enjoys tremendous satisfaction in their relationship with Him. Many people struggling with eating disorders picture God as an angry old ogre, looking for a chance to snuff them out. Their guilt warps their ability to accurately perceive God's love for them.[1]

RECOGNIZE THAT GOD IS AT WORK IN YOU

You've probably seen the bumper sticker that says, "Please be patient! God isn't finished with me yet." You need to hang on to that truth when you're feeling like a nobody—God isn't finished with you yet. He is still refining and fine-tuning you. Philippians 1:6 says, "Be confident of this, that he who began a good work in you will carry it on to completion until the day of Christ Jesus." Be patient with yourself. You have extreme value because the God of the universe is alive in your heart and busy at work in you.

DISTINGUISH BETWEEN WHAT YOU DO AND WHO YOU ARE

Many struggling with eating disorders believe that worth and value come from appearance and achievement. The more perfect they look and act, the greater value they hold. This belief sets them up for an emotional downer because they are pursuing an impossible dream. Perfection can never be attained because being human automatically involves imperfection. The result is a perpetual feeling of never measuring up and never being good enough. (Chapter 5 explains this vicious circle in depth).

Realize that you are more than what you do. Starving or bingeing and purging is only one part of you. You must separate your weaknesses and failures from who you really are. At times your eating disorder may seem all-encompassing, but there is more to you than just an obsession with food. When you're feeling worthless and like you're good for nothing, it might help to pray this way: "God, I feel awful (that's honesty). I really messed up today, but that doesn't mean I'm any less valuable to You. You see all that I can become. You see all of my potential and want to help me grow. Help me to see myself as you see me. Amen."

GET IN TOUCH WITH REALITY

Carlene was ninety pounds and 5'8" tall. However, when she looked in the mirror, she saw a fat person staring back at her. Regardless of what the scales read, Carlene was convinced she was overweight. She had always been ten to twenty pounds heavy while growing up and still saw herself that way. Carlene was now thirty and dangerously thin, but she could not see reality. She saw her reflection through the eyes of her past—an overweight girl who had been hurt and rejected.

"Reality testing" is a tool we use in therapy that helps diminish distorted thinking. When we began to meet together, Carlene's total identity was wrapped up in her ninety-pound figure. She was convinced that people only liked her because she was thin. She believed that if she gained a pound, she would be rejected by her friends. This was a distortion of reality. Somehow, Carlene needed to discover that her friends valued many things about her other than thinness. I asked her to do some reality testing by investigating what her friends and family thought of her.

Carlene left the office that day with a goal for the week to ask her mom, boyfriend, and best friend this question, "What is one thing you like about me?" She was a bit fearful about the assignment, but set her mind to take the risk to ask. Their answers were completely different than she expected. Her mom said she appreciated the compassion Carlene had for others, her boyfriend said he appreciated her sense of humor and laugh, and her sister said she liked the way Carlene listened to her when she had problems she needed to talk through.

Carlene took the risk to test her clouded perception and to believe the feedback others gave her. What a revelation! "Maybe I do have some good qualities. Maybe my weight isn't as important as I thought it was," she told me. By setting this simple goal, Carlene experienced a leap of improvement in her recovery. Getting in touch with reality sharpened her image of herself.

Our perceptions are often inaccurate. Let me encourage you to test your perceptions with others who love you. Don't be afraid to get a second opinion. Reality testing could sponsor a breakthrough in your recovery process.

SHIFT YOUR FOCUS FROM YOURSELF TO OTHERS

Lori came to my office depressed and ready to end her life. She had been bulimic for six years and was weary from the constant wars in her mind. Through the course of therapy, Lori learned she had a tendency toward isolation and complete self-absorption. Obsessed with the way she looked and with what she ate, Lori had lost sight of other people in her life.

One of the goals Lori set in therapy was to move out of her rut of isolation and self-preoccupation. During one week she decided to find one person to smile at and to compliment each day. She also set a goal to extend an act of kindness to one person during the week. At first this was hard for her because she had been so used to focusing on herself, but gradually it became easier. By the fourth week of setting these goals, smiling, complimenting, and helping others actually felt natural.

The interesting byproduct of putting your focus on others is that you as well as they will be encouraged. Don't be afraid to share the kind words and smiles that you have on reserve. Give them out freely and watch the good things that happen.

DON'T PLAY THE COMPARISON GAME

Amy dragged into our support group one night with her head hanging low. She had spent the day at the beach with her best friend and had lost her feeling of self-worth. As the girls basked in the sun, they read the latest glamour magazines. With every flip of a page came a new comparison. As slender models continually appeared, thoughts like, "My thighs are too flabby, my chest is flat, my waist is too thick, my hair is too thin, my nose is too big," bombarded Amy's self-esteem. Amy felt like an overweight failure surrounded by a swarm of success stories.

Comparison will always breed contempt. There will always be people who are more beautiful and more talented than you. There will always be people who are less beautiful and less talented than you. Comparison opens the door to self-pity and sets you up for dejection and gloom. Do you want to tear down your self-esteem? The fastest way to do so is to start looking at other people and comparing your shortcomings to their fine points. I can guarantee that your experience will be demoralizing.

Paul speaks to this issue of comparison in the book of 2 Corinthians. In it he defends his leadership and authority in the church. False apostles had invaded the Corinthian church and were leading people away from the truth of God's message. These false teachers played the comparison game and labored to persuade the Corinthians of their superiority over Paul. In vindication of his position and in response to their comparisons, Paul writes: "When they measure themselves with themselves and compare themselves with one another, they are without understanding and behave unwisely" (2 Corinthians 10:12 Amplified).

The Bible has more to say on this subject. When you're tempted to compare yourself with someone, it may help you to read the sixteenth chapter of 1 Samuel. We read there that all of Jesse's sons were candidates to be king, but only David was chosen. Samuel chose David because God looked into his heart and liked what He saw. This was no selection based on external appearance (verse 17). We learn here that we are not to look at outward appearance or stature because these things are incidental. What is most important is looking at the heart of others. That's the way God relates to us, and that's how we'll find the greatest happiness in relating to others.

One recovered bulimic suggests, "When you look at people, don't allow yourself to give them the once-over. Instead, force yourself to look into their eyes. This is where you'll be able to tap into who they really are." This will guard you from competing in a losing battle. You'll appreciate others more and feel better about yourself, too.

CHOOSE TO CELEBRATE YOUR WORTH

At one point in their lives, Patsy, Rachel, and Jane entertained thoughts of suicide. Their self-hatred overshadowed any hope for recovery from their eating disorder. Fortunately, they chose to ask for help, and in the process of receiving it they learned how to love themselves. All the truths they learned can be yours, too.

When her self-esteem was threatened, Jane referred to the following list of summary statements. She kept them on a paper in her wallet for easy access. When the I'm-a-nobody feeling hits, she chooses to celebrate her worth by focusing on the truths from this chapter.

- God has made me unique. I have the chance to leave a unique mark on the world today.
- I am a competent person with a special combination of strengths . . . but I don't have to be a superwoman who does everything right one-hundred percent of the time.
- I will not allow myself to have a pity-party today—it's a waste of time.
- I will focus on the inner qualities of others today, not on their outward appearance.
- I will reach out to others today and get my mind off myself.
- When I feel like a failure, I will look at my good points and consider my accomplishments.
- When I find a fault in myself, I will recognize it as one part of me, and not equate that one fault with being a total failure.
- I am a great source of pleasure to God today. With that in mind, I'll improve my face value by smiling.
- I realize I don't have it all together, but God redeemed me at my worst and is at work in my life today regardless of what my emotions say.

We live in a fallen world, and feelings of inferiority accompany our imperfection. However, when we build our self-esteem on the solid foundation of what God says about us, we can choose to celebrate our worth on a daily basis. Be encouraged! As you celebrate your uniqueness and your value, your self-esteem will build and you'll be delivered from self-hate.

CHAPTER 4, NOTES

1. Barbara Cook, "Reasons Why I Have Self-Esteem," Bible study presented September 1981, East Hill Church, Portland, Oregon.

THE
PAIN OF
PERFECTIONISTIC
THINKING

For ten years Maria had flip-flopped between weeks of self-starvation and days of bingeing and vomiting or swallowing fifty to a hundred laxatives. At thirty-two, she was convinced she was losing her mind. As a housewife and mother of two children, she felt like a marble on a roulette wheel tossed about by life's frantic whirls. Stability was gone.

One afternoon in therapy, Maria cried, "My kids are driving me crazy with their constant demands. I'm beginning to hate being in the same house with them. I just can't cope. When I wake up in the morning, my arms and legs feel like lead. All I want to do is turn over, bury my head in a pillow, and escape. Steve tries to help with the kids, but he has a lot of demands at work. I hate myself for not being the perfect wife he needs or the good mother my kids deserve. But I can't even handle myself—let alone them.

"I feel pressured to never make mistakes. I can't stand being just average or good. I have to be the best at whatever I do. When I mess things up, I feel like a worthless idiot. At least when I binge I can forget life and bury my frustrations.

"If I could just be a size three, everything would be fine. I know I could handle things and be a better mother and wife if I could lose another ten pounds. My goal is to weigh 100 pounds. Once I reach it, I'll eat normally and have some peace of mind."

Her entire life revolved around eating and exercising. She ran fifteen miles every morning from 4:00 A.M. to 6:00 A.M. while the rest of the family slept. After Steve left for work, she carted the kids to the baby sitter and exercised another three hours at the athletic club.

Maria was plagued by what is often called "the tyranny of the shoulds." She continuously told herself "I should do this better," "I should do more," "I should not have eaten that." These mental conversations were constant. When she exercised she drove herself to do more, and thought, "I should run two more miles;" "I should ride twenty more minutes on the bike;" "I should do another set of repetitions on the weights." I should, I should, I should!

If she ate one small apple (even after five hours of exercise), she felt guilty. "I should have run another five miles. If only I hadn't eaten that apple, then more fat would be burned." Maria was always pushing herself for what she thought was the best—but she could never quite make it because she always felt she should do more.

What happened when Maria "never quite made it?" She fell prey to the lie that she was an incurable, hopeless mass of mistakes. Her own thoughts persuaded her that she was an ugly, unlovable misfit. If she couldn't accept herself, how could anyone else? She didn't feel that God could accept her either. He seemed far away. How could He possibly want to be involved with someone who failed so often? She was certain God was displeased with her. No matter how hard she tried, she never felt good enough.

At the close of one of our sessions, I asked Maria to bring me a list of her "I shoulds." In the back of my mind I anticipated a one-page list with about a dozen items. When Maria returned, she handed me four typed pages of rules and regulations for "living right." Actually, it was a set of externally imposed standards that she had developed over the years to measure up to the expectations of others. Whenever she picked up a cue as to how to please another person, she added it to her list. Her list would be adjusted for one friend and then readjusted for another. Every sermon at church gave her more do's and don'ts to add in order to please God.

Here are some of the beliefs that Maria came up with:

- I must be happy all the time. People don't like grumps.
- I need to wear the latest styles wherever I go so people don't think I'm backward.

- I can't go out of the house without make-up. People don't like "plain Janes."
- I can't gain one pound. No one likes fat women.
- If I'm upset, I need to hide it. Spiritual Christians don't show negative emotions.
- I have to be better than my friends in exercising. Being #1 is the only way to be.
- I have to go to church every Sunday morning and night to please God.
- My house must be spotless. This is a sign of a virtuous woman.
- My kids cannot go out of the house in un-matched clothes. They must have washed hair every day, and never be dirty.
- Meals must always be on time and be nutritious.
- I cannot allow my children to fight. Other people don't like it.
- My kitchen must always be picked up without dishes on the counter or in the sink.
- I must do laundry every day and be caught up with my ironing.
- I should have the house peaceful for Steve when he comes home from work.
- I must get down to a size five. If the models on TV can do it, so can I.

These rules and regulations are only about one-fourth of the ideas on the first page of Maria's list. It went on and on. Just thinking about measuring up to her list makes me tired! And that's how Maria felt . . . defeated and spent. She had no more fight power. Her do's and don'ts had done her in, and she was breaking under the load of perfectionistic thinking.

Maria's mind had been programmed by unrealistic expectations and a need to perform for others. She had learned in the course of growing up that if she behaved in certain ways, she would be loved. If she did what was acceptable in the eyes of others, they would like her. This also filtered into her relationship with God. If she performed well, He would love her. If not, He would reject her. A theology of works and conditional love had seeped into all of her relationships.

Maria spent over a year and a half in therapy with me. Step by step, we dealt with her perfectionism and helped her reprogram her ideas about herself and others. Maria's learning and progress didn't happen overnight. It had taken her years to establish destructive thought patterns, and it took time for her to build a new mindset. The healing needed for perfectionism happens in a deep, gradual, but thorough way.

THE PERFECTIONISM SCALE

How much perfectionistic thinking do you experience in your life? Is your mental vocabulary saturated with "I shoulds" and "I musts?" If you're not sure whether or not you struggle with perfectionistic thinking, you might want to test yourself with the following scale. This inventory lists a number of attitudes or beliefs that people sometimes hold.

Decide how frequently each statement reflects your thinking. Fill in the preceding blank with the number that best describes how you think most of the time. Be sure to choose only one answer for each attitude. There are no right or wrong answers, so try to respond honestly.

—————— 1. If I don't set the highest standards for myself, I am likely to end up a second-rate person.
1) never 2) rarely 3) sometimes 4) often

Pieces of the Puzzle

—————2. People will probably think less of me if I make a mistake.
1) never 2) rarely 3) sometimes 4) often

—————3. If I cannot do something really well, there is little point in doing it at all.
1) never 2) rarely 3) sometimes 4) often

—————4. I should be upset if I make a mistake.
1) never 2) rarely 3) sometimes 4) often

—————5. If I try hard enough, I should be able to excel at anything I attempt.
1) never 2) rarely 3) sometimes 4) often

—————6. It is shameful for me to display weaknesses or foolish behavior.
1) never 2) rarely 3) sometimes 4) often

—————7. I shouldn't have to repeat the same mistake many times.
1) never 2) rarely 3) sometimes 4) often

—————8. An average performance is bound to be unsatisfying to me.
1) never 2) rarely 3) sometimes 4) often

—————9. Failing at something important means I'm less of a person.
1) never 2) rarely 3) sometimes 4) often

—————10. If I scold myself for failing to live up to my expectations, it will help me to do better in the future.
1) never 2) rarely 3) sometimes 4) often

Scoring: Add up your scores. The total may generally be interpreted as follows.

10-20—nonperfectionistic
21-30—average tendencies toward perfectionism
31-40—very perfectionistic

If you scored in the high range, go back and analyze each statement. To which did you respond with "often"? Those statements are your irrational beliefs which need to be challenged.[1]

WEEDING OUT "I SHOULDS"

One of the first things Maria began to work on in therapy was removing the "I shoulds" from her thoughts. She was depressed because she always fell short of her unrealistic expectations. Piece by piece, we examined those expectations and looked for healthy and realistic alternatives.

I encouraged Maria to practice a simple technique called thought recording. In the Bible, God tells us to "take every thought captive" (2 Corinthians 10:4). In other words, we are to be aware of what we are thinking and align our thoughts with Scripture's perspectives. One way to do this is to use a simple thought record chart. This will help you see on paper some of the ways your unhealthy thoughts are tied to unpleasant emotions.

Research indicates that changing beliefs, in and of itself, can often lead to emotional healing. One of the irrational beliefs which occurs most frequently is that all of our undertakings must be done with perfection.[2] By keeping a thought record, Maria was able to discover perfectionistic beliefs that were contributing to her eating disorder and depression. Once she became aware of those thoughts, she began to replace them with healthy perspectives, and her depression lifted.

I need to emphasize that the depression didn't leave all at once. It left in small increments: a little at a time. But it did leave after several weeks and eventually was not a part of Maria's day-to-day life.

Opposite is a copy of the chart Maria used to record her thoughts and moods; it will give you an idea of some of the thought patterns Maria discovered contributed to her eating disorder and depression. (A blank chart has been included in the back of the book. Feel free to to make several copies of it to put in your Personal Growth Notebook so you can begin monitoring your own moods and thoughts.)

As you become aware of the perfectionistic thoughts you have, you'll be in a good position to take charge of those ideas. Awareness is the first step toward change, so take the risk of becoming aware.

THE BLACK AND WHITE MIND-SET

A major characteristic of perfectionism is an "all-or-nothing" mindset in which life is viewed in extremes. Everything is either black or white; there are no gray areas. Something is either a total success or a total failure. I am either a glowing saint or a diabolical sinner. There are no in-betweens.

In the eating disordered, this black or white thinking appears in the area of food, body image, and performance. It is a specific type of irrational thinking that is characteristic of perfectionists. Here are some examples of black or white thinking patterns common to anorexics and bulimics. Rational alternatives are given on the opposite side of the page.

BLACK/WHITE THINKING	HEALTHY RATIONAL THINKING
1. *"I have a list in my mind of safe foods and forbidden foods. I must never*	Sally began to challenge those thoughts with rational ideas like, "I had

THOUGHT RECORD

Date	Situation	Feeling(s)	Automatic Thoughts	Realistic Answers	Outcome
	What were you doing or thinking about when you started to feel like bingeing?	What symptom(s) did you notice (e.g. anger, apathy)? How bad did you feel? (On a scale from 0-100 with zero as "terrible" and 100 as "fine.")	What was going through your mind immediately before you started to feel like bingeing?	How can you answer the negative thoughts realistically and constructively? Is there anything you can do to test out the thoughts or handle the situation differently in future?	How did you feel now that you have tried to answer the thoughts? On a scale from 0-100 with zero as "terrible" and 100 as "fine."
	Sitting on couch in living room after kids left for school, & Dan left for work.	lonely, depressed, hopeless, sad, anxious (80%).	*7 loads of laundry *3 beds to make *toys all over the family room -I want to eat -I want pancakes, bacon, peanut butter, ice cream, twinkies, . . . -windows are filthy with fingerprints -the bathroom is dirty with scum on the tub.	I don't have to do all the house work all at once. I can set a goal to make the beds and do two loads of laundry. Then I will reward myself with a walk around the block and get some fresh air.	still anxious and lonely (50%)

touch the forbidden foods or I'll get fat."

One of Sally's taboo foods was crackers. Any time she ate a few crackers she would go into an immediate binge/purge cycle. After eating six crackers, her perfectionistic thoughts were, "These crackers will make me fat if I keep them down. I might as well binge and then vomit everything."

six crackers which is equal to seventy-five calories. There is no possible way a person can get fat or gain weight on seventy-five calories. So don't worry about the crackers. Enjoy them and get on with the rest of the day."

2. *"I can't eat anything or I'll get fat. Even water is bad because it makes me bloated."*

Terry began to make good recovery when she fought these perfectionistic thoughts with statements like, "It's a good idea to eat something small when I'm hungry. If I keep the calories low, I can have energy without getting fat. I want more pep and strength, so it's O.K. to eat and feel full for a little while. The full feeling will pass and having more energy is worth it."

3. *"When I binge and purge I am a terrible failure and sinner."*

Betsy was constantly depressed by her inability to do things perfectly. She began making good progress in therapy when she stopped punishing herself after a setback of bingeing. She fought her black/white thinking with: "I'm not a total failure. Yes, I did have a temporary set-back, but that doesn't mean everything else in my life is a flop. Every-one makes mistakes. It's part of being human. Would God send His son to die for me on the cross if He thought I was worthless or a piece of junk? No, God sees my weaknesses and yet has promised to walk with me in the healing pro-cess."

4. *"I must be liked by every-one."*

Lucy realized through therapy that she had an insatiable desire to be loved by everyone. When she recognized this as a perfectionistic impossi-bility, it freed her to be herself. Thoughts like these helped her: "I know now that everyone won't like me no matter how nice a person I am. I can't please everyone all the time. It's ridicu-lous to try. The most fun

91

and fulfilling way to live is just to be myself. I'll focus on loving others rather than on being loved."

5. *"I can't stand to have things happen that are different than what I expected. Frustrations are intolerable and should not happen."*

Patsy hated kinks in her schedule. When things happened beyond her control, anger soared. A breakthrough came when she began to think: "I don't like it when unpredictable things pop up, but I can't control everything. Even the best laid plans are often defeated. If I can't change things to improve the situation, I'd better accept it and get on with life."

6. *"I must always be competent, intelligent, and achieving."*

Raylene was a lawyer who felt pressed by her profession to perform with constant excellence. She used self-starvation and binge/purge cycles to keep her weight down. She found freedom when she began to tell herself: "My worth as a human being isn't based on my I.Q. or whether I won my last court case. I have value because God loves me and I am His valuable and precious child, in spite of my abilities to perform. I don't always have to achieve. I don't always have to be competent. It's O.K. to have a nonproductive day once in a while. I have human limitations and fallibilities just like everyone else in the human race."

7. *"I can't have any fat on my body. I must have a perfect figure."*

Cari was a marathon runner and extremely conscientious about her percentage of body fat and muscular tone. She drove herself with abusive exercise to rid her body of any possible fat. She saw great progress in her recovery when she substituted black/white thoughts with, "There's no such thing as a perfect figure. What's perfect, anyway? Not to have any fat on my body would mean death. My body has to have some portion of fat to function properly. Get back to reality."

93

Perfectionistic thinking can bring tremendous pain. It causes us to feel like we're never good enough and always on the brink of one more failure. It paralyzes us and stifles our creativity.

It is important to recognize that black or white thinking doesn't just happen. It is learned. And anything that is learned can be unlearned and replaced in time. All that is required for this to happen is a personal choice, a choice that says, "I'm going to take personal responsibility to discover my perfectionistic thoughts, and then to argue with those destructive ideas, replacing them with healthy, rational ones."

WAYS TO COMBAT PERFECTIONISTIC TENDENCIES

#1. Become aware of some of your own perfectionistic thoughts. Make a list of all the black or white ideas you can recall thinking. (It may help to go back over the examples given by other women in this chapter).

#2. Now go back over the list you just made and pretend that you are somebody else. Write a rational argument against each of the irrational perfectionistic thoughts. Be as convincing and logical as possible.

#3. In order to see how these perfectionistic thoughts have worked against you and your relationships, make a list of the advantages and disadvantages of perfectionistic thinking. Consider these questions: How has black or white thinking helped you? Hurt you? Affected your friendships? Affected your relationship with God? Influenced your peace of mind or anxiety levels? Affected your energy output?

#4. Make a choice. If you want to begin to win over irrational, perfectionistic thoughts, make a contract with yourself to begin now. Say, "I am going to win this battle and I am going to learn to argue with perfectionistic thoughts." If you're serious about this move, read the contract below and sign your name to it.

I, _____, have decided today, _____, to begin a new plan of growth in my life. I am willfully choosing to become more aware of my perfectionistic thoughts (by writing them down as I notice them) and to argue with those thoughts and replace them with rational and healthy perspectives. I realize that I need to relearn how to think in ways that will work for me rather than against me. Each time I replace a black or white thought with a positive, rational statement, I am acting with wisdom and understanding. I can win this battle. I am choosing to move toward healing.

Signed_____

#5. Now, pray over this contract and ask God to give you the wisdom you need to gain insight and to substitute new, healthy ideas for the old, unhealthy ones. Thought patterns can be changed, and God will give you help above and beyond your own abilities.

#6. Use life-giving Bible verses to replace destructive thought patterns. The Bible says that, "The word of God is living and active. Sharper than any double-edged sword, it penetrates even to dividing soul and spirit, joints and marrow; it judges the thoughts and attitudes of the heart" (Hebrews 4:12). As you commit yourself to hiding God's word in your heart and mind, you'll discover a wonderful byproduct. God will begin to point out different thoughts and attitudes that are harmful and that He would like to help you change.

Spend time daily reading and saturating your mind with His truths. Discover the personal promises and golden nuggets just waiting for you in God's love letter to man. As you do, you will be transformed and a new measure of freedom and health will be yours. Then you'll be able to say along with David, "I will walk about in freedom, for I have sought your precepts" (Psalm 119:45).

It's important to remember, though, that God didn't make you a robot; He's not a fairy tale genie in the sky who is going to zap you and make all your problems disappear. Rather, He is a loving Father who offers all His power and resources to you to help you move toward wholeness.

In the book of Romans, God tells us that it is our responsibility to see that our minds are being renewed. This is a constant, ongoing process in which we choose to become aware of our unhealthy thought patterns, and then to replace those ideas with God's ideals. Paul says, "Do not conform any longer to the pattern of this world, but be transformed by the renewing of your mind" (Romans 12:2).

God will help you as you choose to work with Him in transforming your destructive thought patterns. Let me encourage you to ask God to help you learn to think in new ways. He will be faithful to hear your cry and to help you. Psalm 34:15 says, "The eyes of the LORD are on the righteous and his ears are attentive to their cry."

CHAPTER 5, NOTES

1. David D. Burns, "The Perfectionism Scale," *Psychology Today*, (October 1980). Reprinted with permission of *Psychology Today Magazine*, copyright 1980 APA.

2. "Controlling Depression Through Cognitive Therapy," BMA Audio Cassette Publications, New York, 1982.

THE PERIL OF
PEOPLE-PLEASING

"While I was growing up, I desperately wanted to be accepted by my parents. My father is a perfectionist, my mother strong-willed and assertive. My older sister is an extrovert and was always voicing her opinions and criticisms. The stage was set for me. As an insecure younger child, I was always trying to find a way to belong. I deeply desired to please all three of them, and quickly learned that when I agreed with everything they said, they accepted me. To disagree meant rejection, which I avoided in every possible way. My mission in life was to keep peace at all costs.

"I saw constant confrontation between my older sister and my parents. Her honesty sparked friction in our home. It was obvious to me that openness only meant trouble. I decided that I'd be smarter than my sister. My battle plan was emotional hibernation. I withdrew into a shell when any differences began to surface. It worked.

"It worked so well that this is how I formed friendships with others, too. I tried to read their minds, to make sure that what I said was what they wanted to hear. I watched them intently for cues to see what they liked in others, and then tried to conform. I could have easily run away with a National People Pleaser Award had one been offered.

"In college, I actually quit dating a guy when I found out my roommate had her eye on him, too! It was the safe thing to do. I was afraid Karen would reject me if I didn't end the relationship. I was also fearful that Jim would drop me if he knew Karen was interested in him. To eliminate both possibilities, I told Jim I didn't want to date him anymore. But the cost of my emotional hibernation outweighed the benefits, and something in me snapped. I remember crying angrily all night. I hated Karen for liking Jim. I hated everything. My people-pleasing strategy had taken its toll.

"I began to resent the control that other people had over me. I was exhausted from trying to keep everyone happy. I didn't care anymore. I desperately wanted to be myself but was afraid of being different. I had played the game of being what other people wanted for so long, I wasn't aware of a unique identity of my own. I felt trapped in a sea of confusion and found relief through full-blown bingeing."

As you can see in this story, Cynthia had compromised who she was in her efforts to please people. She had allowed others to control her, and when she realized this, she became angry.

At the beginning of therapy, she decided that one of her first projects was to replace the doormat approach to life with healthy relationship-building skills. While growing up, Cynthia had learned to equate closeness and acceptance with agreement, and rejection and alienation with disagreement. This outlook was crippling her. But in time, Cynthia learned that she didn't always have to be be what other people wanted or expected. Today her friendships are solid, and emotional hibernation is buried in her past. The rest of this chapter discusses some of the things she learned about the high cost of people pleasing and the benefits of being herself.

DIFFERENCES ARE A PRODUCT OF UNIQUENESS

"Cynthia was fearful that if she expressed disagreement, others wouldn't like her. Her perspective was limited. What she didn't realize was that she ran the risk of others not liking her because she did not speak up for what she believed.

Can you imagine how predictable life would be if God had made all of us the same? We'd exist like a bunch of clones, talking the same talk, looking the same look, walking the same walk, and life would be a genuine, unadulterated bore.

There are no two people on earth who are exactly the same. It is inevitable that we will have differences of opinion and disagreements with others. Disagreements are as much a part of life as death and taxes. God knew what He was doing when He made each of us unique, according to His perfect plan. We must understand that uniqueness necessitates difference. Difference isn't bad. It's a built-in part of God's plan.

OPEN COMMUNICATION AND HEALTHY RELATIONSHIPS

Our friendships are initiated and developed by the communication we have with one another. If the communication patterns we participate in are destructive or unhealthy, our relationships will suffer. However, if our interactions are positive and constructive, our relationships will be enhanced.

Some basic guidelines for interacting with others can be helpful when you're working on building healthy relationships. Here are some guidelines that Cynthia and many of my clients have found helpful.

DO NOT BE AFRAID TO SAY "NO"

As the head nurse on a very active hospital floor, Carolyn was under constant stress from the demands of others. Whenever any of her nurses needed anything, she jumped. Whenever doctors made unreasonable demands, she smiled sweetly and said, "Sure, I'll be able to do that for you." But underneath she was unhappy and insecure.

In order to feel like she had some control over her life, she became hooked into a routine of self-starvation. During one of our sessions, Carolyn began to uncover the fact that she was using self-starvation to try to regain the control she had given to others. From that point forward, she began to form constructive patterns in her relationships. She began to say no when unreasonable requests were made.

When Carolyn risked saying her first no, she felt clumsy and awkward. She was out of her comfort zone. During those stretching times she reminded herself that if she kept saying yes to everyone's demands, she would snap and end up institutionalized. In order to be an efficient head nurse, she had to say no to some things so that she could keep her priorities in order and be competent in her more important duties.

Paul's counsel in Ephesians 4:15 is wise. He doesn't say, "speak the truth." Instead, he says, "speak the truth *in love*" (italics mine). In other words, be careful and responsible in the ways you make honest statements so that those you're talking to won't be demeaned. Later on in the same chapter, he drives home our need to be loving in our honesty when he says, "Do not let any unwholesome talk come out of your mouths, but only what is helpful for building others up according to their needs, that it may benefit those who listen" (Ephesians 4:29).

Learning to say no is an important part of responsible living. As you act on this truth, you will reap rewards and so will those around you. But remember, always couch your no's in loving explanations that will "benefit those who listen."

TAKE THE RISK OF SHARING YOUR OPINIONS AND FEELINGS

We have a policy at our house to keep short accounts. That means we stay up-to-date with our feelings and find ways of reporting them as they occur. My husband and I are convinced that our relationship will only be as good as our communication.

Sharing negative feelings is sometimes an extra challenge, and the thought of expressing weakness can be uncomfortable. I've seen people sell themselves short by believing that negative feelings are bad, and that strong people don't feel the pangs of deep sadness or anger. But we need to remember that as humans we are made in God's image, according to His likeness (Genesis 1:26). Because we are made in God's likeness, we will experience all kinds of emotions because emotions, both pleasant and unpleasant, are a part of God's character.

As you take the risk of sharing the different perspectives and feelings you encounter through life, you will enrich the lives of others. Don't rob people of the joy of knowing the real you. As you share your feelings openly, you may even discover a wonderful boomerang effect. Psychological research shows that as one person discloses himself to another, the chances are very high that others will reciprocate that openness and honesty. Your transparency can actually refresh others and act as a tool to build bridges rather than walls.

EXPECT CONFLICT AND USE IT CONTRUCTIVELY

Earlier I mentioned that conflict, differences of opinion, and disagreements are inevitable. Remember, conflict is neither good nor bad, it simply is. As you begin to share your opinions and feelings with others, there may be times when you will run into disagreement. And that's OK. Relax with those differences.

Conflict can actually be used as a tool to bring out the best in you and your friends. Proverbs 27:17 says, "Iron sharpens iron, so one man sharpens another." It is through the process of rubbing up against another person's unique character qualities that our lives are sharpened and the rough edges are removed. In conflict I have the privilege of learning new insights and gaining understanding. Without the sharpening process of friction with others, life would be dull. Don't run from conflict. Don't fear it. Don't short-circuit it. Conflict can work for you when you learn to work with it constructively.

In *Caring Enough to Confront*, David Augsburger explains some of the ingredients of constructive conflict.

He says that working through differences by giving clear messages of both caring and confronting is most helpful. Below he lists the various ingredients of constructive conflict. In healthy relationships both caring and confronting hold equal importance. The person interacting must relate in such a way that both ingredients are obvious in the way they communicate.

CARING (and at the same time)	CONFRONTING
I care about our relationship.	I feel deeply about the issue at stake.
I want to hear your view.	I want to clearly express mine.
I want to respect your insights.	I want respect for mine.
I trust you to be able to handle my honest feelings.	I want you to trust me with yours.
I promise to stay with the discussion until we've reached an understanding.	I want you to keep working with me until we've reached a new understanding.
I will not trick, pressure, manipulate, or distort the differences.	I want your unpressured, honest view of our differences.
I give you my loving, honest respect.	I want your caring-confronting response.[1]

DIFFICULTIES WITH CONFRONTATION

Mary worked as an office manager over six executive secretaries. This was an arena where multiple conflicts occurred daily. They came with the territory. She was forever having to settle scheduling difficulties, petty hassles between secretaries, and untimely outbursts by an explosive vice-president.

Mary was also a people pleaser who had a rough time handling conflict constructively. For years she had equated negative emotion with weakness. She had virtually cut off one-half of her emotional spectrum and refused to allow any negative feelings to surface. She had learned a pattern of denying and burying anything unpleasant. After three weeks of working at her job, bingeing and purging became a tool to avoid life's hassles and to relieve bottled anxiety.

At first the binges happened once a week. But they became more frequent the longer she worked at the office. When she began therapy, she was hooked into bingeing and purging eight to ten times a day.

Mary was caught in a vicious cycle. When inevitable conflicts arose, her usual response was to sweetly offer polite platitudes, while anger and frustration seethed beneath the surface. What she didn't realize was that the negative emotions she was hiding were coming back to haunt her in a slow form of suicide—bulimia.

We talked about her work during several sessions and laid some guidelines for handling her conflicts constructively. To begin, she called a meeting with the six secretaries she supervised and gave them each a copy of the caring/confronting list mentioned earlier. She told them that it was important to her that they all work effectively together and that they enjoy cooperative working relationships with one another. Each secretary was instructed to post the caring/confronting list on her desk and to read it twice *before* engaging in any confrontation.

RULES FOR DIFFERENCES

Mary also gave them another list of practical communication rules to follow whenever disagreements or differences arose. This made such a profound impact on the work performance in her department that she was awarded a substantial pay raise. But the benefits didn't stop there. Mary was learning a new way of life. Both negative and positive feelings were being expressed; conflicts were being handled constructively; and her binges were diminishing in frequency and duration.

Maybe you have situations in your life that lend themselves to recurring conflicts. Let Mary's list of rules for disagreement be a tool to help you handle those challenging differences.

Decide on a time and private place to discuss your conflict. Timing is critical. Don't go into a heavy time of weeding out differences when you are ill or emotionally or physically exhausted. Logic is a rare commodity when you are run down. (Proverbs 15:23, "How good is a *timely* word" [italics mine]).

Think before you speak. When emotions are boiling in the heat of conflict, it's easy to blurt out all kinds of tactless remarks. This is harmful to you and others. Before discussing a conflict, take a few minutes to collect your thoughts. It may help to write them down on paper. Seeing things on paper can help you be more objective and rational. (Proverbs 29:20, "Do you see a man who speaks in haste? There is more hope for a fool than for him." Proverbs 21:23, "He who guards his mouth and his tongue, keeps himself from calamity." James 1:19, "Everyone should be . . . slow to speak.")

Set your mind to listen to a different point of view. It takes two to have a difference of opinion. One of the best things you can do to resolve conflict is to be a good listener. Try to tune in to what the other person is saying. Mentally put yourself in their position to find out why they have their strong feelings. As you listen well, you earn the right to be heard. (Proverbs 18:13, "He who answers before listening—that is his folly and his shame." James 1:19, "Everyone should be quick to listen.")

State your opinion clearly and concisely. Don't use loaded words or exaggerated points for persuasion. Simply speak the truth in a kind, loving way. (Ephesians 4:15, "Speaking the truth in love.")

Focus on the present problem. In other words, remain on the topic of disagreement. It's easy to bring up the past and a whole barrage of outdated information when you want to make a point. But this will get you nowhere. Stay in the present and stick to the issue at hand. This will ensure better relationships for today and tomorrow. (Philippians 3:13, "Forgetting what is behind and straining toward what is ahead.")

Do not allow yourself to quarrel and bicker over trivia. Some people just have a knack for bickering. They have a natural way of hooking you into a fight and seem to gain a sense of power by manipulating you into an argument. These kinds of interactions are not worth your time or energy. It's best to politely excuse yourself rather than to fall prey to power-hungry tactics. (Proverbs 20:3, "It is to a man's honor to avoid strife, but every fool is quick to quarrel." Proverbs 17:14, "Drop the matter before a dispute breaks out.")

Relinquish your rights to change others. Your calling in life is not to agree with everyone or to try to make them agree with you. Remember, uniqueness necessitates difference. Appreciate the uniqueness of others and give them space to differ from you. Work at forming relationships with a mixture of different types of people. Variety is the spice of life. (1 Corinthians 13:5, Amplified Bible, "Love [God's love in us] does not insist on its own way, for it is not self-seeking." 1 Corinthians 13:7, Amplified Bible: "Love . . . is ever ready to believe the best of every person"—even when there are strong differences of opinion.)

When someone wrongs you, don't hold a grudge. As human beings, we are imperfect. We all make mistakes. During the next few months of my life there will probably be somebody somewhere who will say something that will hurt my feelings. The same probability is true for you as well. When hurtful remarks fly in your direction, don't allow them to become a cancer of bitterness in your heart. This will only magnify your anguish and pain. Forgiveness will get rid of bitterness and will allow your emotions to heal. (Colossians 3:13, "Bear with each other and forgive whatever grievances you may have against one another. Forgive as the Lord forgave you." Proverbs 17:9, "He who covers over an offense promotes love, but whoever repeats the matter separates close friends." Ephesians 4:32, "Be kind and compassionate to one another, forgiving each other, just as in Christ God forgave you.")

Tell others, "It's OK to disagree." There are times when you will hold a completely different opinion from someone else, regardless of lengthy discussions and debate. That's fine. Simply tell your friend you realize that you both feel strongly about the issue, that you respect her position, and that it's OK for the two of you to disagree. Then part company peacefully. (Ephesians 4:2-3, "Be completely humble and gentle; be patient bearing with one another in love. Make every effort to keep the unity of the Spirit through the bond of peace.")

Trying to live by the motto "peace at all costs" is destructive. People pleasing taken to the extreme leaves a person exhausted, empty, and floundering in identity confusion. There is no possible way you can please all the people in your life all the time. It's irrational to think that you can even come close.

God has made you a very special individual. Celebrate your individuality. Take the risk of openly sharing the real you with others. You are God's gift to your friends and family, and they are God's gift to you. Lavishly enjoy your similarities and deeply appreciate your differences. Both aspects are important parts of God's plan.

CHAPTER 6, NOTES

1. David Augsburger, *Caring Enough to Confront* (Ventura, Calif.: Regal Books, 1980), p. 15.

THE
ENTRAPMENT
OF SECRECY

It's 2:00 A.M. Your family has been asleep for hours, but you're awake, lying in bed thinking through every item in the refrigerator. You give up trying to sleep, crawl out of bed, and sneak down the stairs to the kitchen. The next hour is a blur as you consume all the leftovers and sweets you can find.

Gathering together all the cartons and wrappers, you stash the evidence in a trash can so no one will notice. Next you force yourself to vomit so that the food won't turn into pounds. Feeling numb and dizzy, you tip-toe back up the stairs and climb under the covers once again. Your husband startles you suddenly, saying, "Is everything all right?" You reply, "Everything is fine. I just had to go to the bathroom."

You feel guilty because you know he'd be concerned if he knew about your consistent bingeing and purging. Openness and honesty were values that you both agreed were vital to your relationship—and yet here you are, lying again. As you try to go to sleep, you find yourself praying the same old prayer you did the night before: "God, there's got to be more to life than this senseless routine. Forgive me for lying. I'll never do it again."

LYING, STEALING, AND SECRET RITUALS

Most everyone I've counseled about eating disorders has had to deal with secrecy and dishonesty. It is as much a part of the disorder as food. Many bulimics take exhaustive steps to cover up their bingeing. Lying, stealing, and secret rituals are woven into their daily routine.

Lindsey shares her experience: "During the five years of my first marriage, my husband never uncovered my closely guarded secrets. No one knew. Covering my tracks was a part of my daily routine. Lying about food was second nature to me. For example, for several months I went to the same grocery daily to buy large quantities of binge food. I told the checker I was a nursery school teacher buying snacks for the children."[1]

Judy was involved with a different form of secrecy that paralyzed her family relationships: "For thirteen years I was anorexic. My children never saw me eat a meal until two months ago. Stan always asked me to eat with the family, but I refused. Family food wasn't a part of my 'safe foods' or a part of my ritualized routine. To keep peace, I told them I had eaten so much fixing the meals, I couldn't eat with them during mealtime. I lied through my teeth. My regular routine was to starve myself all day, and then at 11:30 P.M. have a salad, yogurt, and an orange after everyone else was in bed. I hated the lies, but I was so comfortable with my rituals that I did anything to hang on to them."

Lying is not the only form of secrecy that accompanies eating disorders. Research shows that that twenty-four percent of those with eating disorders steal compulsively.[2]

Anna and Melanie were part of that percent. For years they shoplifted consistently. "We had been best friends all through high school and we wanted to go to a Christian college together. So we did. Our first year we were roommates, and that's when we began to eat pizza at midnight. Both of us started gaining weight. We were really depressed one night after consuming a giant full-combo pizza and decided to figure out a plan to get skinny again. We had tried the vomiting route, but hated it because it was too hard and never worked real well.

"Our new plan was to try Ex-Lax and diet pills. We wanted more pep for studying, and we knew diet pills were loaded with caffeine. So we hopped into the car and drove to the nearest drugstore. We searched the aisles and found the Ex-Lax and diet pills but were too embarrassed to take them to the cashier. We thought she might tell someone from school what we were doing. Stuffing the pills into our coat pockets, we bought nail polish to make it look like we had found what we wanted. All the way back to school we rationalized our dishonesty. 'They'll never miss one bottle of Ex-Lax and one package of diet pills. They have so many things in that store, what's the difference? Besides, we're only going to try our plan for a week. We can pay them back through buying more of the things we need from their store rather than somewhere else.'"

But the stealing didn't stop that Friday night. A week later when their supplies ran out, they were back in the drug store doing the same thing. Gradually the laxatives and diet pills lost their effectiveness, so they had to double the amounts. One package of each item eventually turned into seven. Binges are expensive, so to cut costs they began to steal their favorite binge foods. They knew when store managers were off duty and developed elaborate schemes to steal high-cost foods when there were only a few employees in the store. This continued through their college years.

After four years of compulsive laxative abuse, diet pill consumption, and stealing, Anna and Melanie had established some strong behavioral patterns. Could life ever be different for them? Could they be free from the stealing and pill-popping? The answer is "You bet!" They are free. It took some decisive action and hard work, but they'll be the first to tell you, "It's worth every bit of effort to live in freedom rather than in bondage!"

DEALING WITH DISHONESTY

How did Melanie and Anna break free from the destructive chains of dishonesty and secrecy? By taking responsibility for their actions. When they were willing to acknowledge and admit that they were stealing, Melanie and Anna took a major step toward freedom. While talking with someone they trusted, they confessed the deception that had been a regular part of their daily interaction with others. This admission opened the door for their friends to support them and to hold them accountable.

Next, they chose to change. They repented. Repentance occurred when they made a 180-degree turn and chose to walk in the opposite direction away from their former behavior. Melanie and Anna determined to stop stealing. They stopped rationalizing and recognized that their actions were destroying them.

Melanie and Anna made a commitment to themselves and to each other to consciously work on only speaking the truth. They made a pact to not even tell "little lies." But they didn't stop there. They went a step further and prayed to God for added strength to be transparent and to quit hiding behind secret rituals. They also committed themselves to pray daily for one another to be open and truthful.

When they risked vulnerability, they began to get well. Being honest with others became more important than being liked by others. An exciting byproduct of their commitment to transparency appeared. Their friends began to invite them out more often and told them how much more they appreciated the real Anna and Melanie. As a result, they were able to build deeper and more meaningful relationships.

I love the way God's Word teaches us about truthfulness. While teaching in the temple one afternoon, Jesus said, "If you hold to my teaching, you are really my disciples. Then you will know the truth, and the truth will set you free" (John 8:31-32). The principle here is that truth brings freedom. Christ came to set us free and to help us walk in the light . . . in the truth.

WHAT GOD SAYS ABOUT DISHONESTY

When you are replacing an old behavior with a new one, it helps to keep a list handy of a variety of self-statements concerning that new behavior. Some of my clients who have learned to become transparent and open about their eating disorder compiled a list of Scriptures that helped them make their about-face from dishonesty. Read through them. Perhaps they'll help you, too.

- God and man respect honesty. Proverbs 3:34, "Do not let kindness and truth leave you; bind them around your neck, write them on the tablet of your heart. So you will find favor and good reputation in the sight of God and man."
- Cling tight to a truthful lifestyle. Proverbs 23:23, "Buy truth and do not sell it, get wisdom and instruction and understanding."
- God will help you be truthful and honest. John 16:13, "But when he, the Spirit of truth comes, he will guide you into all truth."
- To be good at loving others, be truthful. First Corinthians 13:6, "Love does not delight in evil but rejoices with the truth."
- Use mental discipline to concentrate on honesty. Philippians 4:8, "Whatever is true, whatever is noble, whatever is right, whatever is pure, whatever is lovely, whatever is admirable . . . think about these things."
- Honesty will keep your conscience clear and allow you to have peace of mind. Acts 24:16, "So I strive always to keep my conscience clear before God and man."

God's Word gives us principles to help us live honestly. One of my favorite verses in the book of James is, "Confess your sins to each other and pray for each other so that you may be healed" (James 5:16). God knows the profound impact confession can have in our lives. He knows that as we take personal responsibility for our faults, we take a step toward healing. As we commit ourselves to change and then pray with others, we take another big step toward healing. And each step we take, God is there to back us up one hundred percent. Don't let the entangling chains of secrecy and dishonesty keep you in bondage. Take a risk. Repent. And then watch new dimensions of freedom add a refreshing vibrancy to your life.

CHAPTER 7, NOTES

1. Lindsey Hall and Leigh Conn, *Understanding and Overcoming Bulimia: A Self-Help Guide* (Santa Barbara, Calif.: Gurze Books, 1982), p.9.

2. Regina Casper, "Bulimia: Its Incidence and Clinical Importance in Patients with Anorexia Nervosa," *Archives of General Psychiatry* 37 (September 1980).

YOUR
VIEW OF
YOUR
SEXUALITY

"When I feel fat, I don't feel sexy. And I feel fat all the time. My husband is always bugging me to have sex with him. He says I look just fine, but I don't believe him. I know I'm overweight and I feel unattractive. Sometimes I give in to him, but I just hate it because I'm so self-conscious. He only says those nice things because he's trying to seduce me."

Susie, a young wife and mother, had been bulimic since she was in high school. She became disgusted with sex not long after her marriage and soon-to-follow pregnancy. "I love my baby, but being pregnant made me fat! I binge and vomit now to maintain my weight, but that twenty extra pounds I gained with the baby isn't coming off. To be honest, sex is just not as important to me as food and my weight. Sometimes I'm afraid that having sex may lead to another pregnancy—and more weight. I panic when I think about getting fatter.

"I've told Rick to wait until I've lost the extra pounds so I'll feel better about myself. I won't mind being available to him when I'm thin again. But he's getting sick of waiting. He tells me he's attracted to other women who flirt with him at work. I get scared that he might have an affair, but the truth is, I just don't care about sex anymore. I can't even relax enough to have orgasms.

"Rick points out that my Mom and sisters seem interested in sex with their husbands. He doesn't understand! It's easy for them. They're not obsessed with food and weight the way that I am. They're thin, so they don't have to worry about being sexy. Besides, I'll bet they never have fantasies about chocolate sundaes the way that I do. I would much rather have dessert than sex any day!"

YOUR SEX DRIVE IS AFFECTED BY YOUR EATING DISORDER

Susie's feelings are not unusual. Many women with bulimia and anorexia nervosa have difficulty becoming sexually aroused. They feel self-conscious, unattractive, and unable to give themselves sexually to their husbands. I've heard many say, "Once I lose weight and get over my eating disorder, I'll be ready to have sex." Thoughts of food and preoccupation with thinness diminish sexual drive and squelch romantic thoughts.

One doctor found in his research that masturbation and sexual fantasies and impulses either cease or become much less common in eating disorder patients. One of his subjects said, "I have fewer sexual feelings than a sick oyster!" The results of his study showed that the anorexic's sex drive often dips far below normal. [1]

You may struggle with the same conflicts Susie faced. If you find that your sexual identity is being buried by your eating disorder and food, then this chapter is for you.

POSSIBLE REASONS FOR SEXUAL INHIBITIONS

I talked with Susie at length about her lack of interest in sex. As she was open about her feelings, she began to discover some reasons for her apathy. Here are some of the things she learned in the process.

Self-esteem is important for a good sexual relationship. Susie realized she could not express herself sexually because she did not like herself. Anorexia nervosa and bulimia erode self-esteem. Many times the devastation is so severe that the woman is left hating herself. It is extremely difficult to give yourself to someone in a sexual relationship when you don't like what you have to offer.

Preoccupation with thinness and food also diminishes interest and enjoyment in sex. Susie confessed, "I am just too busy thinking about food to worry about sex. When I do give in and have sex with my husband, I'm thinking about what I can sneak from the kitchen later. Or if I've just eaten, I'm feeling guilty about my calorie intake. I couldn't care less about orgasms. I feel too guilty about my bingeing to become aroused."

I would like to add here that a good sexual relationship requires openness and sharing. However, while intimacy may be desired, it is often feared by the woman who is trying to hide her disorder. Because of the secrecy involved with an eating disorder, she often feels shut off from her closest contacts. In order to regain a feeling of closeness, she may continue to try to meet her husband's sexual needs, but find that she is unable to call up her own desires.[2]

A person's *body image* also influences sexual feelings. Most women with eating disorders have distorted body images—and Susie was no exception. Five feet six inches tall, she weighed 120 pounds and believed she was overweight. Although her friends and family told her she looked fine, she viewed herself as fat. Her body image was distorted.

Much of my time with Susie focused on rebuilding her perception of her body. She needed to realize that thinness does not equal sexiness. Before she could experience healthy sexual feelings again, she had to take a hard look at her sexuality and how it was constructed.

HOW YOUR VIEW OF YOUR SEXUALITY IS FORMED

We can think of sexuality as being made up of three facets:

- how God sees your sexuality—which is found in Scripture

- how you see your own sexuality—which is hidden deep in your preferences and self reflections
- how others see your sexuality—which is often based on society's definitions and standards

When we diagrammed Susie's view, it looked like this:

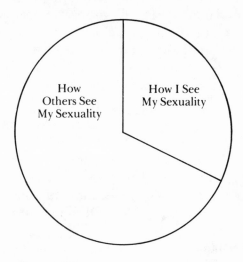

The whole circle represents a person's sexuality. As the diagram indicates, Susie's perception of her sexuality was composed predominantly of what others thought. Their comments and observations influenced her perspective the most. Susie talked about some of the comments she had internalized: "I saw my mother fight to stay thin all her life. Mom felt unattractive after eating one dessert. My sisters wanted to look like the wispy and willowy models in *Seventeen*. I hated having to compare myself to them, but I believed them when they said I had to lose weight to catch a boyfriend."

As you can see from the diagram, only a small portion of Susie's view of sexuality was based on her own self-reflections. God's view played no part in her perception. She had used society's definition and standards and others' feedback as the primary building blocks to construct her view of her sexual self.

There is a major problem with this pattern. Outsiders don't always have an accurate perception of the real you and don't always give the best or healthiest feedback. Although others can help you identify your blind spots, there are things about yourself that only you and God know. God is the only One who can give you an objective and unbiased view of who you are and how you can be sexually healthy.

SOCIETY'S DISTORTED VIEW OF SEXUALITY

Susie's view of her sexuality was heavily influenced by reading *Seventeen*, *Glamour*, and *Vogue*. When she looked in the mirror, she compared herself to the models in the bathing suit ads. Of course she never measured up.

She had adopted the impossible standards set by the media. It's interesting to see how those standards have changed within the last twenty-five years. In 1965, when Twiggy won her way into the spotlight, our culture announced that thin was beautiful. Until then, our role models were full-bodied women: Donna Reed, Elizabeth Taylor, Debbie Reynolds, and Annette Funicello. They had an abundance of curves. But today, New York modeling agents would probably tell someone who looks like Marilyn Monroe that she's chubby.

The message that "Fat equals failure. Skinny equals success!" has been burned into the minds of American women. When asked why they want to be thin, most anorexics and bulimics answer: "Because I'm supposed to be!" From Mom to Madison Avenue the message rings out loud and clear. What society doesn't realize is that this warped and perverted message is actually killing women at alarming rates. It's time to wake up to the insanity of our culture's "ideal" image.

Cleverly and subtly the media communicated to Susie that unless she looked like the models who were constantly being paraded before her, she was overweight and unattractive. If they could convince her (and others like her) that she needed to lose weight, perhaps she would buy their product.

Advertising companies have manipulated many of us into feeling that we "need" certain products. They work hard to create a market for their product—which at present may not be perceived as a necessity. The advertising campaign for Tab is a good example of a marketing strategy that attempts to create a need. When Tab was introduced to the market, not many of us were stocking our cupboards with diet drinks. Then we were bombarded with ads and billboards of good-looking people with slender, young bodies. The accompanying slogan read, "Drink Tab, it's for beautiful people."

Madison Avenue created an image that women wanted to identify with: A thin, perfectly groomed woman in a bathing suit with several handsome men hovering around her. If drinking a diet cola meant looking and living like that, it was worth the price (even with saccharin!). The subtle message was quite clear.

Unfortunately, many women respond to the Madison Avenue message the way one of my clients did. Emily shared her feelings one day in my office. "I can't even watch one commercial without getting a sick feeling in my stomach. I want to look like those women, but I'm big boned. I know I'll never look that good. I'll never be attractive or have a good relationship with a man. The only thing that makes me feel better is pizza, ice cream, and sandwiches. I hate bingeing and purging, but it helps me forget how ugly I feel."

Another client who was in the competitive world of high fashion modeling put it this way: "Even if you have all the right features and carry yourself perfectly, you can never be thin enough. After shows, all of us are exhausted and starved, so we go out for Italian food or to a smorgasbord and binge for hours. The pressure of the fashion show wears off while we eat and talk. Then we all go to the restroom and throw up so we can be slender the next day. Everybody knows 'you can never be too thin or too rich.' All the girls I know in modeling want both!"

We are told we are not sexy unless we are thin. Jane Fonda, Cathy Rigby, Cherry Boone O'Neill and others have talked about this pressure to be thin and how it drove them to bulimia or anorexia nervosa. This pressure to always look good often makes women self-conscious, tense, and unable to relax with their sexuality.

THE BODY I ONCE HAD!

Many women with eating disorders try to avoid maturing physically. Ellen remembers the ages of ten to twelve with great fondness. "I was innocent and pure. My body was perfect. My breasts and hips had not developed, and I was as thin as a broomstick. I remember how agile I was. I loved gymnastics, could do all the routines perfectly, and felt fantastic in leotards.

"When I turned thirteen, everything was ruined! I started my periods and my breasts and hips filled out. It seemed like curves and clumsiness hit together. Pimples and boyfriends all came at once. Life got so confusing. Why did I have to grow up?"

Life was easier for Ellen as a pre-adolescent. There were no sexual conflicts and very few boyfriends to break her heart. The pounds didn't cling as easily to her body when she overate. One afternoon Ellen reflected on her past, saying, "As I grew older, boys stopped being my friends. When my body developed, they began to relate to me differently. I didn't get as many hugs and I felt less attractive. Ever since then I've felt clumsy around guys. I don't feel put together as an adult, especially when it comes to my sexuality. I can't just run up and give people hugs like I used to when I was a little girl. They take it all wrong. My affection is interpreted as a come-on instead of as spontaneous caring. I don't like being an adult woman. Life was a lot more fun as a skinny little girl."

Ellen and I talked about her attractive qualities as an adult woman. In time she learned appropriate ways to express love and affection. She also began to use cards, notes, and a pat on the arm when outward affection seemed awkward or inappropriate.

We also did some reality testing about her childhood. Since Ellen recalled only positive memories, she talked to her mom to gain a more balanced view of her past. One of the negative aspects of her childhood that was brought to her attention was all the rules that she hated as a ten-year-old girl. Eventually, Ellen was able to identify many of the freedoms she enjoyed as an adult woman. She began to realize that she would never want to sacrifice those joys by living in the past. She learned that the fond memories of her pre-teen body could remain, but she needed to feel good about her mature body, too.

Ellen desired a thin, pre-adolescent body because she did not want to deal with sexual conflicts. Other women who feel that thin is beautiful crave thinness because they are convinced that thinness equals sexiness and beauty, and they long to be sexy and beautiful. While these may seem to contradict each other, both are valid and present in eating disorder patients. Your view may be somewhere in the middle, depending on how you felt about your sexuality when you were growing up and how you have internalized society's standards.

CHANGING YOUR PERCEPTION OF YOUR SEXUALITY

Even if you have some misconceptions about your sexuality, you can gain a new and healthy view. You can be free to enjoy your sexuality as God intended. God designed you to be a sexual person with feelings and desires. His view is positive and whole. If you align your view with God's view, you will have dignity and sexual self-esteem based on a solid foundation. God's view of your sexuality can become the reference point for your view of your sexuality.

In order for Susie to build a healthy view of her sexuality, she turned off the TV for a while, canceled her favorite women's magazine subscriptions, and began to focus on her inner qualities. First Samuel 16:7 came alive to her: "The LORD does not look at the things man looks at. Man looks at the outward appearance, but the LORD looks on the heart," and she began to channel her thoughts in the direction of her unique personality characteristics rather than on her outer appearance. She also joined an exercise class a couple of nights a week and a Bible study once a week.

While she realizes she can't avoid the media's skinny images forever, Susie is beginning to like herself and to feel less threatened by society around her. She feels more attractive and freed from old distortions—but she had to block out the media's distorted message for a while before she could see herself clearly.

God's view of you is quite different from society's. But it is possible to align your view of sexuality with God's view rather than with society's unreasonable standards. The following diagram shows a more desirable way to build your view of your sexuality.

This is the chart Susie and I drew after months of counseling.

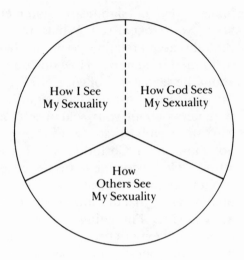

In this second diagram, God's view is a major part of Susie's perception. The section representing other people's view is greatly diminished. A blending of God's view into Susie's view is represented by the dotted line.

Susie was able to change her perception of her sexuality as she spent time studying what God says about beauty and sex. Two of the Scriptures she studied in order to understand God's view of sex were 1 Corinthians 7 and Song of Solomon 4:1-15. She also found it helpful to read a few books that dealt with the issue of sexuality from a biblical perspective. Three of the books she enjoyed most were *Christian, Celebrate Your Sexuality* by Dwight Small, *I Married You* by Walter Trobisch, and *Intended for Pleasure* by Ed Wheat.

Change also happened in Susie as she took some of the steps below. If you are not happy with this area of your life, you might like to try some of the following suggestions. They may help you move toward a more balanced view of your sexuality.

1. Make a list of significant statements about your sexual self. What are your thoughts about relating to your husband or to men in general? How do you feel about the sexual side of yourself?

2. Make a second list of God's significant statements about your sexual self. You can start with a study of Song of Solomon and 1 Corinthians 7. For example, "God made me in his image and pronounced me *very good*." Or "Song of Solomon says that our love is better than a fine wine. I'm going to savor this lovemaking experience." Or "God made me a sexual person and 1 Corinthians 7 says not to avoid coming together. Good sex can be a part of my marriage, even while I am recovering from this eating disorder!"

3. How do these two lists differ? At what points are you off base?

4. Choose to believe the truth of God's Word and healing perspectives rather than the destructive lies of impossible societal standards.

5. Try to become more aware of your sexual feelings rather than denying them or covering them up with food. Don't bury those feelings. Learn to get in touch with them instead.

6. Begin to look at your body as a *good* creation by God—regardless of weight loss

or weight gain. Focus on your good points rather than your imperfections.

7. Try not to let perfectionism invade your sexual relationship. Don't expect yourself to be a perfectly performing lover. There will be great times as well as "not so great" times, just as there are victories and failures in your eating habits. Be realistic with your expectations so that you're more comfortable with your experiences.

8. Try to break out of the secrecy mode of your lifestyle. Your spouse needs to know your thoughts and feelings. Try to communicate your sexual needs and preferences to him. He's not a mind reader, so tell him what you like and don't like—in both verbal and non-verbal ways.

9. You will have to begin to pay attention to internal cues once again. Your body has sexual needs just as it has hunger pangs. Try to begin to listen to your body's sexual impulses. This will help you grow in your ability to receive and give love.

10. Try to begin to *relax* with your sexuality and enjoy life. This may seem impossible to you. You may be fearful that your sexual feelings are gone forever. Let me encourage you. The sexual feelings are probably still there—they've just been quenched. It may help you to do some exercises which focus on your senses and feelings in order to rediscover the sexual side of yourself. *The Gift of Sex* by Clifford and Joyce Penner details some of these exercises for you.

OLD PATTERNS DIE HARD

Susie will be the first to tell you that it takes time to change. But after several months she learned new and creative ways to relate to her husband and to enjoy her sexuality. She made a choice not to let the fifteen extra pounds she carried drive a wedge into her marriage relationship.

Even though it is difficult to come out of the closet and to be honest about your eating problem, it is worth it! If you're married, I encourage you to be open with your mate. Tell him what you need and like. If you're single, ask God for male friends who will affirm you as a woman without sexual expectations. You have a positive sexual self hiding inside. Share it! Celebrate it!

Perhaps you have denied your sexuality or put it on permanent hold so that you can work on your eating disorder. This tunnel vision will limit healing to only one area of your life. Don't put off working on changing your view of sexuality just because you are trying to overcome an eating disorder. You can work on both areas at the same time and experience the great joy that comes with multiple steps of growth!

You are a complex person, like a diamond with many brilliant facets. Your sexual facet can shine bright and clear as you learn the truth about who you really are. The more you understand God's love for you, the easier it will be for you to love yourself. God will help you move toward wholeness. You can learn to give and receive love unconditionally, without fear of rejection. With God's help, all of these things are possible. It will just take time and a cooperative effort with Him.

CHAPTER 8, NOTES

1. A. Keys, J. Brozek, A. Henschel, O. Mickelson, and H. L. Taylor, *The Biology of Human Starvation* (Minneapolis: University of Minnesota Press, 1950).

2. D. M. Garner and P. E. Garfinkel, *Anorexia Nervosa and Bulimia* (New York: Guilford Press, 1985).

THE
VALLEY OF
DEPRESSION

"I don't know what's the matter with me. I feel hopeless. Yesterday when I was sitting at the breakfast table, I couldn't even muster the energy to walk across the kitchen to get the sugar bowl. When it came time to fix dinner last night, I stood in front of the freezer for twenty minutes watching the food defrost, incapable of deciding which vegetables to serve. Nothing seems to matter anymore."

Sandy's symptoms had become obvious. She was depressed. "I have no zest for life anymore. All I want to do is binge or sleep the day away. It's like being stuck in a dark cave without knowing how to escape."

Sandy is like many other eating disorder victims who experience deep valleys of depression at some time during the eating cycle. A bulimic will usually get depressed immediately before or after the binge/purge cycle and the anorexic right after eating. During this time even the smallest tasks may seem monumental.

Although depression varies from mild to severe, there are several key symptoms that represent the experience we label depression. Here are some of the signs to watch for:

- feeling blue or sad
- disturbed sleep patterns
- weight change (loss or gain)
- loss of interest in life
- indecisiveness
- discouraged or despondent feelings
- irritability
- loss of appetite
- guilt feelings
- social withdrawal

In one study eighty percent of the bulimics were depressed and in another fifty percent of those with anorexia suffered persistent depression.[1] Eating disorders and depression are often inseparable companions. One reinforces the other. For example, Sandy's depression sometimes hit hard in the morning when she first woke up. Thinking about the responsibilities of the day overwhelmed her. In order to avoid the excessive demands she placed on herself, she binged. The food relieved her emotional pain temporarily, but after bingeing and purging, guilt and depression set in. The more she binged, the gloomier she felt. The deeper she sank into depression, the more she binged. Sandy was caught in a vicious cycle.

WHAT CONTRIBUTES TO DEPRESSION?

Since many seek to escape depression through bingeing or starving, it's important to identify some of the factors that contribute to depressed feelings. Depression doesn't happen in a vacuum. If you have been battling despair, it is probably due to a constellation of factors. Let's take a moment to identify some possible contributors to depression.

Anger turned inward. I've had many clients tell me they are angry with God for allowing them to have an eating disorder—but they are afraid to tell Him how they feel. Others are disappointed with their parents because they are unable to help. Many are angry with themselves because of how they feel. Each unexpressed and unresolved irritation fuels the simmering fire within. Instead of venting their frustrations, they swallow them with junk food and deny their anger.

Perfectionism and guilt. Many perfectionists battle depression because they find it impossible to meet the demands they place upon themselves to be a supermom, superathlete, superwife, and supercareer-woman. A cloud surrounds them for days when they fail at something they feel they should achieve.

Hopelessness about life. After many futile attempts to try to overcome an eating disorder, some of my clients have felt they would never get better. They do not want to live because they do not believe their situation will

137

change. One client told me, "There's no light at the end of the tunnel. With food consuming all of my time and energy, life isn't worth living."

Physical imbalances. Many times hormonal and chemical imbalances will trigger depression. Jackie told me, "Just before my period, I crave chocolate and sweets. So I indulge. Then I feel worse. I know that it is just my time of the month, but my binges seem uncontrollable when my emotions take such a huge dive."

Lack of control. When circumstances seem uncontrollable, and you are unable to influence what is happening around you, depression can set in. With many of my clients the desire to be independent clashes with their inability to control their eating habits. When someone tries to tell them how they should be eating, the feeling of lack of control is compounded.

Loss of someone or something important. This is one of the more obvious causes of depression. Terry was able to look back and identify the day she lost her job as the point when she lost her enthusiasm about life. Three weeks after she left work, she found herself in a deep sea of depression. "When I lost my job, I thought I would love having free time. But all I want to do is eat or sleep. I feel like I'm not worth anything anymore."

Ongoing high stress. Continual pressure can make you feel overwhelmed and unable to cope. When Valerie came to see me, she felt like she was going to explode. She said, "My husband argues with me all the time about why my bulimia isn't subsiding. He says if I'd just try harder, I'd get better. Between arguments with him and stresses from my job, I feel like I live in a pressure cooker. It catches up with me emotionally and I cry a lot. I've had it with the whole situation."

Lack of meaning. Disillusionment takes the excitement out of living. Gail could find no purpose in her existence and was beginning to believe that living wasn't worth her time or energy. "Why doesn't anything I do make a difference? My life is so routine; I just go through the motions. Nobody would care if I wasn't here anymore. If I could do something really great, then I could feel good about myself again."

Low self-esteem. I have never met a person with poor self-esteem who did not battle depression. Mindy told me, "I can't think of one thing I like about myself— inside or out. I wish I could be somebody else. My eating is just one of the rotten ways my real personality comes out. I don't like who I am."

As you can see, the things that contribute to depression are varied and numerous. Through counseling, the eating disordered can discover specific things that contribute to their feelings of despair. Understanding these factors is the first step toward growth and change.

It's important for me to add that the contributing factors mentioned in this chapter are not as cut and dried as they appear. All of them interact with each other. For example, the first five may work together at the same time in one person. Let me illustrate.

Ellen wants to be a long distance runner and sets an impossibly high goal to run 100 miles a week. She is a perfectionist and believes she should be able to reach her goal. When she can't, she feels out of control and binges to cope with her failure. Frustrated with her obessions, she becomes angry. As she hides these negative feelings behind artificial smiles, her emotional energy is drained. It isn't long before a sense of hopelessness kills her dreams for becoming a marathon runner. In order to cope, she decides to set more unreasonable goals . . . and the cycle begins again. Can you see the pattern? Unreasonable demands lead to failure. Failure leads to the feelings of frenzy and lack of control. Frenzy leads to bingeing and purging, which leads to anger and depression. Hypoglycemia magnifies Ellen's problems even further because of the sugar imbalances in her body.

139

It may encourage you to know that understanding the "whys" can lead to the development of specific strategies or "how to's" for getting well. With these insights and your God-given capacity to understand your behaviors and emotions, you can change.

HELPS AND SOLUTIONS FOR DEPRESSION

I know of no one who is immune to depression—especially those who struggle with an eating disorder. So what can be done? Are there pathways out of the valley of depression?

The answer is yes! The medical and professional counseling fields use many different approaches for treating depression. The list is as limitless as a person's creativity. These tools are all helpful, but must be developed around the specific problem being faced.

Some people, for example, experience depression simply because of chemical imbalances in their body. Treatment for them needs to begin with medication and blood sugar balancing. Without this taken care of first, they could have the best therapy available and still not recover emotionally. Once physical imbalances have been ruled out, it's possible for a person to begin to use specific strategies for alleviating their depression.

When Sandy began counseling, I asked her to have a complete check-up immediately after our first session. Blood tests revealed that she was diabetic and needed to take insulin. Once the medication stabilized her blood sugar, she began to feel great relief from depression. After that, she was in a much better frame of mind to tackle her eating disorder. In counseling she began to try to get in touch with the thought patterns surrounding her depression. She also set goals concerning her behavior so that she wouldn't reinforce sad feelings. It was important to consider each of these factors.

We can think of the tools for coping with depression as falling into three categories: tools that help us with our thoughts, tools that help us with our actions, and tools that help us with our bodies. Let's look at each of these categories in turn.

TOOLS FOR DEALING WITH THOUGHTS

Depression limits one's ability to think clearly, and many times a depressed person's options seem very limited. The thinking processes become so negative that hope is extinguished or at best minimal. But when negative thoughts are changed, feelings can become more positive.[2] Feelings and behaviors most often follow a change in thinking. Here are several techniques that can help you change your thinking.

Try thought stopping. One tool for dealing with depression is thought stopping. Sandy used it to eliminate thoughts that were depressing or self-defeating. As mentioned earlier, Paul tells us in 2 Corinthians 10:5 to "take every thought captive." In other words, we are to be aware of what we are thinking and line up our thoughts with Scripture's healthy perspectives. Thought stopping can help us do this. As soon as an unwanted thought occurs, say "Stop!" Say it sharply and clearly in your mind or out loud. Then substitute a different thought in place of the unwanted one. This substitute thought should be the opposite of the unpleasant one.

Sandy, for example, spent an evening bingeing and purging. Afterwards, her mind was filled with self-deprecating, guilty thoughts. She hated herself, was angry, and felt out of control and hopeless. Her journal reflects her thoughts: "I hate myself for what I've just done. I wasted a whole evening, plus my parents' food money. I've fallen back into the trap I worked so hard to crawl out of. I was doing fine until I decided to take a bath to relax. The women's magazines I read in the bathtub started me on a comparison trip. I'm so homely compared to those models. I'll never be that thin or beautiful, so why bother trying?"

In time, Sandy learned to say "Stop!" to that kind of thinking. When she read magazines, she fought against the self-defeating thoughts with statements like, "I don't have to look like those models. Besides, no one looks that good without a lot of help from hairdressers, make-up artists, and fancy lighting techniques. I can be happy with myself because I'm loved by God and have His Spirit within me."

Instead of berating herself for a setback in her bingeing and purging, she learned to think these types of thoughts: "Stop! So you blew it. You don't have to let it ruin the rest of your week. Let it go. Forget it. Talk to God about it and wipe your slate clean. Look at the hours ahead as a new opportunity."

Check out your internal dialogue. Try monitoring your thoughts for a while by using a thought record chart. Do your thoughts include positive statements about yourself? Try to counter your negative talk with statements that God has made about you in Scripture.

Use prayer as a means of changing your perspective. Focus on God's adequacy rather than on your inadequacy. Pray as if God were in the process of changing you (He is!). Let someone else pray for you who is not loaded down with your situation like you are. A friend's prayers will be more positive, and you need their emotional support.

Stop disqualifying the positive. There are positive aspects to your life. Let them be as large as the negative aspects. When you look in the mirror, look at your warm smile or sparkling eyes instead of your waist or hips. Everyone has negative and positive characteristics. When you only emphasize those you don't like, you discount the good. Pay attention to what is terrific about you. God made you with some great qualities. Don't ignore them—enhance them!

Test the reality of your thoughts in some objective way. Is your perspective warped by your depressed feelings?

Check out your thoughts and see if they line up with God's Word. Or analyze your views with a friend. It's possible to have tunnel vision and blind spots and not even know it.

Sally's starving episodes intensified when her boyfriend dropped her. In order to gain a clear perspective, she asked a friend who had known her for a long time to help her out. "Do you think I am independent enough to make it if John doesn't come back to me? How was my life before I met him? Would you help me focus on the other aspects of my life that are worth living for?" Sally needed her friend's opinions to help her see that she could live without her boyfriend. As the fog cleared, she was able to feel more relaxed about the break-up, and gradually started eating more healthfully.

Face your thoughts of anger, don't deny and bury them. Anger is powerful and it can be destructive. It just depends upon how you deal with it. Some people express anger by kicking, swearing, screaming, bingeing, purging, starving, and throwing themselves into fits of rage. This does bring results, but they are frequently less than rewarding!

A more beneficial way of dealing with anger is to express your angry thoughts to God, or perhaps to a trusted friend. As you face those thoughts with their help, you're likely to experience a release from the fiery feelings that accompany those ideas.

One of the most dangerous things you can do is harbor bitterness in your heart. Hebrews 12:15 says, "Watch out that no bitterness takes root among you, for as it springs up, it causes deep trouble, hurting many" (TLB). Ephesians 4:26 says, "If you are angry, don't sin by nursing your grudge. Don't let the sun go down with you still angry—get over it quickly" (TLB). In other words, God is telling us that for our own health, it's best to keep short accounts and to get rid of grudges on a daily basis!

143

Be careful with introspective thoughts. Insight can help people overcome their depression, but it can become dangerous if it moves beyond healthy insight into obsessive introspection. It's best to limit introspection to therapy sessions or perhaps to periods of time when you're talking with a friend. Don't try to figure everything out. When you're depressed, you're most likely to be overly critical and overly hard on yourself. Obsessive introspection will drain your emotional reserves and can intensify depression [3].

TOOLS FOR DEALING WITH ACTIONS

Just as depression narrows thinking, it also frequently narrows a person's activities. The feelings reinforce the behavior and the behavior reinforces the feelings.

Sandy's friends noticed that she had drawn into a shell and wouldn't go out with them any more. This is a typical pattern seen among depressed people. The more Sandy stayed at home, the more she wanted to be left alone. Increased isolation brought increased depression and decreased her opportunities for climbing out of her despair.

When she came in for counseling, she knew something had to change. Her life had turned inside out so that everything she saw was like a photographic negative. Where there should have been joy, she felt only sadness. Where life with its continuing promise should have sustained her, only the oblivion of death attracted her. Living had become hell on earth.

Through the course of therapy, Sandy began to take action. You've heard the phrase, "It's easier to act yourself into a new way of feeling than to feel your way into a new way of acting." I know—it sounds simplistic. But it works! And Sandy is one person who experienced the reality of that truth.

I frequently encourage those who are depressed to set action-oriented goals on a weekly basis. They start

144

with baby steps. Gradually it becomes easier for them to place one foot in front of the other and to persevere in their journey out of despair.

Several action-oriented goals that I've used in counseling have been particularly helpful to those suffering depression. I'd like to pass these on to you, hoping that they'll assist you in recovering, too.

Each morning when you wake up, commit your day to God. When the alarm clock rudely interrupts your sleep, try to make these the first words out of your mouth: "Thank You, God, for this day. I commit it to You, and ask You to work in my life in a new and fresh way. Even though I feel crummy, I believe that You'll be with me and that You'll help me through the day."

Plan a time each day to read God's Word. Jesus said, "The Spirit gives life. . . . The words that I have spoken to you are spirit and they are life" (John 6:63). When your feelings are saying that death is a good option, your mind and your spirit need to provide a rebuttal. As you spend time in God's Word, the Holy Spirit within you will speak to you words of life and health and strength. He will help you gain new insights and fresh glimpses of hope as you ask Him to encourage you during that time of reading. Set aside a special time each day to get alone with God. He will always be more than ready to meet you there!

Try to establish a daily routine. When you're depressed, it's easy to flounder through the hours of the day and to lose touch with any structure or routine. But a clumsy and muddled approach to your day can actually reinforce your depressed feelings.

I encourage depressed clients to try to establish some sort of a routine that brings them satisfaction. At first this may mean simply getting out of bed at the same time each morning, showering, and dressing. Then they might set a specific time for going to bed each night, and choose a project to work on in the afternoon. Structure and order can bring emotional relief.

145

Try to get involved in caring relationships. Being with people who nurture you can help you feel better. When was the last time you were with someone who cares for you? Laughter and feelings of being loved and valued are excellent therapy for depression. All of us need people who love us. Although it's easier to withdraw, I encourage you to try to reach out to others. Try getting together with one person during the week or calling a couple of friends on the telephone. A little TLC from a friend can really boost your day.

Try to get adequate rest. This is a necessity for coping with depression. Are you getting your solid seven to eight hours of undisturbed sleep? If not, exercise may help you to rest better (but don't overdo it). Relaxation training may also help your brain to switch off, enabling you to sleep. Have you tried deep breathing or muscle relaxing exercises? You might like to get in touch with a local hospital and ask them to send you some information on relaxation exercises.

Incorporate exercise into your daily routine. Exercise can sometimes lift one's perspective quicker than other remedies. A brisk walk, a short jog, jumping rope, or aerobic dance may bring about renewed hope and energy—as well as get your circulation going.

Some doctors are now prescribing regular exercise programs for depressed patients and finding excellent results. Mood elevations occur during exercise because as the body exerts energy in a workout, endorphins are released in the brain. These endorphins are the body's natural tranquilizers and antidepressants. And believe me—they're a whole lot cheaper than behind-the-counter drugs.

Plan pleasant events. You may have found yourself trapped in a downward spiral. One doctor observed that depressed people are notorious for hibernating and focusing on their sad feelings.[4] They forget to participate in fun and playful times. Victor Hays has made a long list of what he calls "pleasant events." He suggests that every depressed person needs to experience pleasant events that boost their ego and give them a chance to be involved with positive social experiences and strong feelings. He points out that it is impossible for any of these three things to co-exist with depression. Take a look at some of the pleasant events he offers. The more of these you can incorporate into your lifestyle, the better you'll feel.

Meeting old friends

Participating in a lively discussion

Completing a task in my own way

People watching

Observing animals

Doing a really good job on something

Expressing affection

Having coffee with a friend

Learning a new skill

Planning a special project

Giving my opinion when asked

Acquiring new knowledge

Making new friends

Having time to do whatever I want

Being with a loved one

Having pleasant thoughts about friends or loved ones

Having sexual relations with my spouse

Going out for lunch or dinner

Paying someone a compliment

Expressing myself clearly

Eating a good or special meal

Wearing something special

Laughing

Wearing clean clothes

Going to a party

Participating in strenuous activities

Going to a play or concert

Contributing my time or money to a charity

Camping in the mountains

Going to the library

Participating in a sports event (e.g., tennis, golf, football)

Buying something for myself

Playing cards, bingo, or group games

Working on a problem

Participating in a church activity

Setting a realistic short-term goal

Cheering for my team or favorite player

Playing pool

Making something from leather or sculpting

Dancing

Going places where there are many happy people

Listening to beautiful sounds (the wind, a waterfall)

Going on a date

Competing in a sports event

Giving a present

Writing a letter

Bathing or taking a shower

Attending a meeting or lecture

Cooking a special meal

Taking a picture

Looking for interesting things (rocks, driftwood)

Watching a sunset, sunrise, or special cloud formation

Hearing a funny story or joke

Telephoning a friend

Being with family

Doing something nice for someone

Swimming

Playing an outdoor game like frisbee

Reading something special

Going to a Bible study

Listening to music

Gardening

Thinking about an interesting problem or topic

Watching a fire

As I said earlier, depressed people tend to focus on their sad feelings and let all the pleasant activities of their life fade away. I encourage you to fight this tendency.

Your actions are extremely important to how you feel. Just as some actions will make you feel worse, others will give you a boost. The action-oriented goals I've shared in this chapter have helped many clients find a way out of their depression. Committing your days to God; reading His Word; establishing a routine; caring for others; and scheduling time for rest, exercise, and pleasant events are some of the things you can do to find relief from depression.

As you incorporate some of these things into your life, chances are you'll feel more like smiling. Whether you are in the planning stage or actually participating in these goals already, a change of behavior will bring positive results. Involvement with life around you brings a sense of hope.

We've looked at some ways to work with thoughts and actions in the midst of depression. Now let's consider one final aspect of treatment: body chemistry.

TOOLS FOR DEALING WITH BODY CHEMISTRY

Most of the time changes in thinking and behavior patterns will relieve depression. However, some new studies are finding physical connections between depression and eating disorders. In one study, seventy-six percent of the bulimics treated improved with anti-depressant medication.[5] The improvement included less bingeing, less purging, less depression, and more self-control. Now that's progress!

Depression and eating disorders appear to be interwined at many levels. Even though the relationship is not fully understood, we must not ignore the possibility of the physical aspects involved.

Megan found that her depression did not leave even when her eating behavior improved. "I have been in black moods as long as I can remember. When other kids played on the playground, I sat alone under a tree and felt sad. I thought about my life a lot and decided that I would never fit in. My mother and grandfather always seemed down to me, too. I talked to Mom and she said that depression runs in our family.

"I'm sure that my bulimia did not help my moods, but even after I stopped bingeing and purging, I was still depressed. I went to see a Christian psychiatrist whom my counselor recommended. After a complete medical evaluation, she put me on a low dosage of antidepressants. For the first time in my life I feel alive. I can wake up in the morning rested and excited about what God has in store for me. Unless God does a miracle in my body chemistry, I will probably be on antidepressants a long time. After all these years of blaming myself, I was sure surprised to find out that a major part of my depression was biochemical."

Like Megan's, your depression may be more than just a simple case of the blues. Treatment for biological depression may require rebalancing your system's chemicals through medication.

As a Christian counselor, I often have to address the concerns of Christians who question the use of medication for a problem that is perceived as simply emotional. What they fail to realize is that many times depression is caused by a chemical imbalance in the brain and nervous system. It seems strange to me that the same people who are uncomfortable with antidepressant medication usually feel fine about using anticoagulants to treat heart disease or using insulin to treat diabetes.

Research has shown that antidepressants are successful in curbing the intensity of depressed feelings. God can use medication to bring healing just as He can use a miracle. The medical and psychiatric communities are making great progress in the research and treatment of eating disorders and depression. Let's not ignore what they have to say.

Knowing that there are specific factors that contribute to depression can help you accept and deal with the feelings that result. Whether you are most helped through changes in thinking and behavior or through medication, the important thing is that you use the tools that work best for you.

A good starting point for getting out of depression is to pray, "God, help! Give me strength today as I take responsibility for my emotions. Help me put one foot in front of the other, and to do everything in my power to get out of this pit!" Then reach out and ask for help from someone who knows about eating disorders and depression.

As you call on God, you allow Him to intercept you at your deepest point of despair. As you turn to Him in your weakness, He will channel light into your darkness, and He will help you find ways to win your battle.

God knew you would experience the sting of emotional pain and suffering in this world. With that understanding, He offers the encouraging words that He has "overcome the world." So in the midst of your humanness, He can reach into your life and help you stand on your feet again. He can bring peace to your turmoil, order to your chaos, and hope to your despair. God loves you. Be encouraged, for He has promised to walk with you completely through the valley of depression.

CHAPTER 9, NOTES

1. G. Garner and P. E. Garfinkel, *Anorexia Nervosa and Bulimia* (New York: Guilford Press, 1985).

2. Jerry Schmidt, *Do You Hear What You Are Thinking?* (Wheaton: Victor Books, 1981).

3. Ibid.

4. Peter Lewisohn, Ricardo Munoz, Mary Ann Youngren, and Antoinette Zeiss, *Control Your Depression* (Englewood Cliffs, N. J.: Prentice-Hall, 1978).

5. J. E. Pope and J. I. Hudson, *New Hope for Binge Eaters* (New York: Harper and Row, 1984).

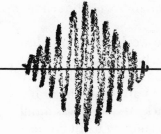

YOUR
BODY
TALKS

Whenn I first began counseling Stephanie, she brought in her diary full of stories about her eating disorder. Some of the entries talked about the fears and problems she had concerning her body. One excerpt included the following writings.

April 15: I'll never forget this week and the terror that came when my body collapsed. On Monday I bought a box of laxatives, sleeping pills, and diet pills. I was scared to death that the cashier wouldn't let me buy them, but she just gave me a strange stare over her coke-bottle glasses and rang up the bill.

I had decided once and for all that I was going to lose the ten pounds of excess baggage I was packing around. I stopped eating and drank just enough water to swallow my pills. It worked! The weight dropped quickly and every morning I woke up three pounds lighter. I was ecstatic until some weird things started happening.

Five days into my fast my heart started frantically pounding and skipping beats. Then one afternoon I fainted in class. When the nurse at school revived me, I was so dizzy that I couldn't walk on my own. She sent me home.

A few days later my whole world caved in. Mom came in to wake me up for school, but I didn't wake up. I had completely lost consciousness. The next thing I remember is waking up in the hospital, feeling like I had just been run over by a Mack truck. My body was numb and it took all the strength I could muster to lift my head off the pillow.

That was the day I met Dr. Franks. By then I was desperate. I needed some answers. With some feelings of panic, I cried to Dr. Franks, "I'm scared. What's happening to me? I'm afraid I'm going to die and I'm only seventeen!"

Stephanie is one of many eating disorder victims who experience physical problems as a result of abusive eating habits. Bulimia and anorexia had taken their toll on her body. Medical researchers have found that there are several physical ailments common among those who starve, binge, and purge. This chapter is designed to help you become aware of some of those problems. As you continue to read about Stephanie's hospitalization and discussions with Dr. Franks, it is my prayer that you'll gain insight about how your body works and how it talks to you.

Stephanie's discussions continued with Dr. Franks: "I've binged and purged at least once a day since I was a junior in high school. Sometimes the guilt was so intense after bingeing that I starved myself for three or four days.

"About six months ago, I stopped having my menstrual periods. I was really concerned after several months passed. Each month I felt like I was going to start, but I never did. Last month I finally had a period, but the cramps were so violent I couldn't get out of bed for three days. Four Tylenol didn't put a dent in the pain.

"I'm also worried about the crazy headaches I get each week. My head throbs so badly, I feel like it's going to explode. Usually I get dizzy spells, too. The combination of the pain and the spinning sensation scares me. Why does my body betray me like this?"

In response to Stephanie's cry for help, Dr. Franks spoke honestly with her. "Stephanie, you can rest assured that we can help you. Your failure to menstruate, your cramps, and your headaches are ways that your body is talking to you. It's saying something is wrong and that you need to get some help. I'm glad you came to talk to me about all this. I'm here to help you, but in order to do so I need to be honest with you.

"I don't want to scare you, but I do want you to realize that ignoring your body's warning signals could be fatal. According to the latest medical journals I've read, five to ten percent of people with eating disorders starve to death.[1] You have lost more than twenty-five percent of your normal body weight. That's partly why your mother couldn't wake you up yesterday and why you ended up here in the hospital.

"I know that you have never talked to anyone about your eating disorder, but I need to know all the symptoms that you have been experiencing. Start at the beginning and tell me about the symptoms you first noticed."

CRAVINGS

For the next hour Stephanie and her doctor discussed the physical changes her body had been going through. Beginning with a description of her eating patterns, Stephanie admitted, "An average binge for me could be as much as a dozen donuts, two bags of cookies, a quart of ice cream, and several candy bars. When I binge, I feel a sense of relief from my problems. But about a half an hour later, I'm in agony because my stomach is so stuffed. Vomiting usually brings relief. But this last year I noticed that the gnawing hunger and craving for sweets returned just a few minutes after purging. That's the first time I recognized that my strategy was beginning to backfire."

Dr. Franks explained that craving food is typical after huge binges on sugar.[2] "After bingeing, your body begins the digestion process. Your pancreas sends out insulin to help balance your blood sugar. In addition to aiding the digestion of sugar, insulin helps transport an amino acid called tryptophan into the brain. Once in the brain, tryptophan is rapidly transformed into the powerful neurotransmitter serotonin. Increased levels of this hormonelike agent cause a feeling of calmness. This is the 'binge calm' that follows the consumption of rich, sugar-laden foods. That's why you feel a sense of relief and a temporary escape from your problems and worries.[3]

"But when you vomit, you interrupt your body's sugar-balancing cycle because no food is left to be digested. The insulin that has been released has nothing to work on. The excess insulin in your blood stream causes more hunger pangs. Instead of leveling out, the insulin level drops, so your body craves more sugar.

"Your pancreas and digestive system were not designed to handle all these mixed messages and ups and downs. It's as if you are sending it two opposing signals at once. One says your stomach is full, the other says it's empty. That's why you are hungry even though you've just eaten. The more you binge and purge, the more your body will experience cravings."

IRREGULARITY

"It's hard for me to talk about this, but sometimes my body goes for several days without a bowel movement. My stomach gets so bloated, I can hardly get my pants zipped. It feels like my insides are going to burst. The only way I get relief is by swallowing a box of laxatives. After that I'm fine for a few days, but then the constipation returns. Every once in a while I use enemas because laxatives are so expensive."

Stephanie didn't realize that the laxatives were wreaking havoc on her intestines. Unfortunately, laxative abuse and enema abuse is common, even though these have been proven ineffective as diet tools.[4]

In response to Stephanie's complaints, Dr. Franks said, "When you use laxatives, you run the risk of enlarging your bowel. When the bowel enlarges, muscle control is lost, and this prevents the bowel from functioning properly. No doubt you experienced episodes of extreme diarrhea. It may help you to know that your intestines and bowels are muscles. Like any other muscle, they need exercise to work properly. Right now your bowels depend on chemicals to stimulate them into action. They don't know how to function on their own.

"When you starve yourself, this process is complicated even further. Your digestive process comes to a grinding halt because there is nothing for the intestines to digest.[5] Then when you do eat again, your system is sluggish and doesn't know what to do with the food. Since your intestines haven't been working for a few days, it takes time for them to get moving again. That's why it takes so long for the food to work its way through your system and why you feel so plugged up.

"The good news is that in time your system can learn how to operate on its own again. Once you resume normal eating patterns, your bowel will probably readjust. It will just take time and patience on your part."

For the first time in her life, Stephanie was beginning to understand the warning signals sent by her body. It was such a relief to get some answers. The time spent with Dr. Franks was invaluable. His compassion helped her feel comfortable, and she was able to honestly share her fears and physical problems with him. Their conversations continued.

MENSTRUATION

"I tried to sweep all my other symptoms under the rug, but when my periods stopped and didn't return, I really got worried! They were off and on for a couple of months, and then they stopped completely. I'm afraid I'm so messed up, I won't be able to have children some day."

Dr. Franks shared some research about the menstrual cycle. "When a woman's fat levels drop below twenty-two percent of her normal body weight, her menstrual cycle stops.[6] Like yours, the fat level of most anorexics and bulimics is beneath this cutoff, and so periods often cease. Once you gain enough weight and are out of the danger zone, I suspect that your periods will straighten out, although it may not happen right away. But I can't be certain about your fertility and ability to have children. One out of six American couples experiences difficulty conceiving[7]—and their inability to conceive is often not complicated by an eating disorder. I've read studies that seem hopeful for anorexic women and others that are not. More research needs to be done in this area. For now what is most important is that you take some serious steps to getting your body back in balance. At least that way you'll know you're doing everything in your power to ensure the possibility of a future pregnancy."

ELECTROLYTES

Dr. Franks went on to say, "One of the biggest concerns I have with my bulimic patients is the possibility of electrolytic imbalance caused by starving and purging. Forty-nine percent of all bulimic patients have disturbances in their electrolyte levels.[8]

In response to Stephanie's question about the meaning of the term *electrolytes*, Dr. Franks replied, "Electrolytes are minerals such as calcium, phosphorus, chloride, sodium, potassium, and magnesium. They balance with the water content of the body and carry electrical impulses for your body.[9] If any of these becomes depleted through vomiting or laxative or diuretic abuse, the disturbance causes severe problems. A low potassium level, for instance, can lead to irregular heartbeat and even death. Electrolytic imbalances can make your muscles feel weak and cause fatigue. I've seen cases of kidney failure due to dehydration from electrolytic imbalances. It's possible that an imbalance of this sort contributed to the dizziness and fainting spells you mentioned earlier.

"Some endocrinological testing can determine how healthy you are in these areas. If I find through testing that your system is depleted of these chemicals, I can help you with supplements. But more important, you can help yourself regain balance through healthy eating. We can work together to get your body back to normal."

HEART PROBLEMS

Stephanie, stunned by what her doctor told her, painfully replied, "I had no idea my eating disorder would cause me so much pain and so many problems down the road. I always thought being thin meant being healthy. Instead, so many things are going wrong with my body that physically I feel I'm falling apart.

"I've noticed lately that my heart has been skipping beats and that I feel short of breath. That panics me because I have always had a strong heart. Why would bingeing and purging affect it?" Stephanie asked.

"You have to realize, Stephanie, that your electrolytes affect the electrical impulses which regulate your heart rate. Many of the anorexic and bulimic women who die suffer the consequences of cardiac arrest from electrolyte imbalances.

"Your heart can only take so much strain. You put a lot of extra pressure on your system when you exercise too strenuously, binge and purge, starve, and use laxatives. Your irregular heart rate, or arrhythmia as it's called, is a serious sign that your chemistry is out of balance."

Stephanie learned a great deal about her body during her time with Dr. Franks. It became obvious to her that her eating behavior needed a drastic turn around. She had come to a crossroads. Her abusive eating patterns were killing her, and the only options left were change or death. Fortunately, she chose to change.

In the months ahead, Stephanie gathered more facts about the physical problems that often accompany eating disorders. Some of the information came from the support group she attended during her three months in the hospital. Further understanding came from talking with nurses and reading articles and pamphlets. In the remainder of this chapter I've included some of the other things Stephanie learned about her body.

THYROID

Eating disorder victims often complain about exhaustion and fatigue. Sometimes this lack of energy can be caused by a thyroid deficiency. Thyroid is a hormone produced by the thyroid gland which regulates the body's energy levels. When the body does not receive food for a few days, less thyroid is produced, so the energy level drops. The body decreases the amount of thyroid it produces in proportion to the amount of weight lost. Some eating disorder victims ask for thyroid pills, hoping that it will boost their energy levels.

Most doctors who work consistently with the eating disordered won't prescribe thyroid medication because it only masks the symptoms and does not treat the eating disorder itself. When balanced eating patterns and a healthy weight is maintained, thyroid levels usually return to normal and energy levels equalize.

LANUGO

Another symptom frequently experienced by anorexics is lanugo. Not only does thyroid affect energy levels, but it also helps regulate the body's temperature. When a person's weight dips below normal, insulating fat is lost. A person is likely to feel cold most of the time if fat levels are below normal or if the thyroid is out of balance.

In an effort to keep warm, the body grows a downylike fuzz, called lanugo, which covers the skin. You may have seen lanugo on newborns. It is just a temporary covering that disappears once normal fat levels are attained. This is a protective step the body takes to keep it from reaching dangerously low temperatures. It fights to keep warm.

DETERIORATION OF TEETH

The bulimic who has binged and purged for years usually experiences dental problems because acid from the gastric juices stimulated in vomiting erodes tooth enamel.

Unfortunately, cavities and erosion are permanent, but when vomiting stops, further damage can be prevented. The teeth of many bulimics become discolored, being brown or gray in appearance. A good dentist can evaluate what type of damage has been done and offer assistance in cosmetic improvements. Some dentists start eating disorder patients on fluoride treatments.[10]

SWELLING

It's not uncommon for an eating disorder to disturb the body's water balance. Anorexics and bulimics often experience swelling in their feet, hands, glands, and face. This is because vomiting or laxative abuse usually leads first to dehydration and then to excessive water retention.[11]

Swelling, or edema as it is sometimes called, gets worse for a short time after purging stops. This bloatedness is temporary and is another way the body tries to return to normal functioning. Eventually the body's chemistry balances out and sheds this retained water naturally without diuretics.

CLOSING COMMENTS FROM STEPHANIE

"It has been two years since I was released from the hospital. I thank God for people like Dr. Franks who were honest with me about my problem. Today I'm no longer imprisoned by an eating disorder, but my healing didn't come overnight.

"At first the fast weight gain scared me. When I stopped taking laxatives, my legs swelled from water retention to the point that my ankles were as fat as my thighs. I couldn't walk for three days. Fortunately the swelling was temporary. After about a week or two my body began to shed the excess water on its own without the help of diuretics. By the end of my first month in the hospital, I ate three meals a day and didn't purge. It was good to feel like I was beginning to control food rather than having it control me."

LISTEN TO YOUR BODY!

Stephanie's physical problems came after years of starving, bingeing, and purging. Her experience is not uncommon. Perhaps you have noticed that you have some of the signs and symptoms that have been mentioned in this chapter. Stephanie will be the first to tell you that it is extremely important to seek medical advice and support on these issues. You need to be aware of symptoms and complications involved with anorexia and bulimia. Ignorance is harmful and dangerous. Your body talks. Listen to what it is saying!

Paul pointedly asks, "Haven't you yet learned that your body is the home of the Holy Spirit God gave you, and that He lives within you? Your own body does not belong to you. For God has bought you with a great price. So use every part of your body to give glory back to God, because He owns it" (1 Corinthians 6:19-20, TLB). Glorifying God includes taking care of your body and having a healthy view of food. It means listening to your body's warning signals. Only you really know your body. It's your responsibility to do the best you can to work with God in keeping your body well. As you take steps to begin to care for your body, God will help you. He desires to see your body operating in balance.

CHAPTER 10, NOTES

1. J. E. Pope and J. I. Hudson, *New Hope for Binge Eaters* (New York: Harper and Row, 1984), p. 49.

2. William Duffy, *Sugar Blues* (New York: Warner Books, 1982).

3. Peter Nash, M.D., "A Matter of Fat," *Shape* Magazine, March 1985, p. 142.

4. G. Bo-Lynn, C. A. Santa-Ana, and J. S. Fordtran, "Purging and Caloric Absorption in Bulimic Patients and Normal Women," *Annals of Internal Medicine* 99: 14-17.

5. Wallace Hodges, "Physiological Implications of Eating Disorders," *Hopeline Newsletter*, vol. 3, no. 5.

6. Rose Frisch and J. W. McArthur, "Menstrual Cycles: Fatness As a Determinant of Minimum Weight for Height Necessary for Their Maintenance or Onset," *Science* 185: 949-951.

7. Judith Stigger, *Coping with Infertility* (Minneapolis: Augsburg Publishing House, 1983).

8. J. E. Mitchell, R. L. Pyle, E. D. Eckert, D. Hatsukami, and R. Lentz, "Electrolyte and Other Physiological Abnormalities in Patients with Bulimia," *Psychological Medicine* 13: 273- 278.

9. Patti Burkey, R.N., seminar on electrolytic imbalance, Mt. Tabor Family Practice Clinic, Portland, Oregon, December 1984.

10. D. M. Garner and P. E. Garfinkel, *Anorexia Nervosa and Bulimia* (New York: Guilford Press, 1985).

11. C. G. Fairburn and P. J. Cooper, "Self-Induced Vomiting and Bulimia Nervosa: An Undetected Problem," *British Medical Journal* 284: 2253-2255.

PART
3

THE BATTLE
CAN BE WON!

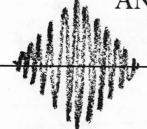

HOW
CAN I EAT
NORMALLY
AND NOT GET FAT?

I n his book *Diets Don't Work,* Bob Schwartz cites some amazing statistics. He says, "Do you know how many people actually get the results they want by dieting? One out of every two hundred! The failure rate of diets and weight loss programs is 99.5 percent. Out of every two hundred people who go on a diet, only ten lose all the weight they set out to lose. And of those ten, only one keeps it off for any reasonable length of time."[1]

I wholeheartedly agree with Bob—*diets don't work.* Yes, there are hundreds of diet books on the market. New fad diets are coming out each month, and people are buying the new releases, even though they have twenty-five other diet books in their library that "didn't work for them." There is a desperate longing in the hearts of many to find a quick method for weight control.

Many anorexics and bulimics believe the misconception that crash dieting is an effective and fast way to lose weight. Anorexics practice crash dieting on a daily basis by fasting and avoiding most foods. Bulimics practice crash dieting tactics on a regular basis following bingeing. Most of those who struggle with eating disorders have tried every crash diet on the market and have experimented with a wide variety of diet pills and diet aids. However, there is a crucial factor concerning these rigid patterns that must not be overlooked.

In their efforts to lose weight quickly, those who suffer with eating disorders rarely realize that the critical issue is not *how many* pounds they lose, but *what kind* of pounds they lose. When pounds on the scale decline, this can be due to fat loss, water loss, or lean muscle tissue loss.

The loss of muscle tissue is serious and dangerous. "Low calorie diets—less than eight hundred calories per day—can accelerate the rate of muscle loss by increasing loss of body cell mass along with fat loss. The loss of lean body mass occurs as soon as extreme dieting begins. The ability to repair the loss of lean body mass decreases as age increases."[2] Crash dieting throws off the balance of lean body mass and body fat.

Some medical professionals believe that continued starving, bingeing, and purging slows down your body chemistry so that more fat is stored and less is burned. In short, the extreme weight loss patterns that accompany anorexia and bulimia are a setup for a failure in long-term weight control. Starving, bingeing, and purging are not the answer to keeping weight off for life. These techniques may work for a season, but the long-term effects can go in only two directions: a fatality or the yo-yo syndrome which leads ultimately to further weight gain.

YOU CAN EAT NORMALLY

For some reason the anorexic and bulimic often feel that the more restrictive or rigid they are with their diet, the more successful they'll be controlling their weight. However, the opposite is true. The more restrictive their diet, the more likely they are to go off of it and fail. It's necessary to make an important point here. If you are struggling with an eating disorder, you have to make a choice. *You have to choose whether you want to continue to fight against seeing a certain number of pounds on the bathroom scale or whether you want to learn to eat normally and experience long-term weight control. You cannot invest yourself in both directions.*

If you choose to remain obsessed with weight loss, the destructive chain of food's grasp on your life will tighten. However, if you choose to channel your energy toward learning how to eat normally, several positive byproducts will be yours: increased peace of mind, stabilized eating patterns, and a chance to begin effective and lasting weight control.

I remember sitting with Karen one afternoon and explaining that anorexia and bulimia were not effective

171

forms of weight control. She understood what I said, but with despair cried, "I've had this eating disorder for eight years and I don't think I'll ever be able to eat normally again." I have heard those words so many times in my office from clients. Karen and many of her struggling counterparts feel doomed to a life of lettuce and celery, or to vomiting and laxatives after eating sweets or fattening foods. With great joy, I can say that Karen has proven her statement wrong, and for the first time in many years she eats normally.

Karen's recovery began the day she made that critical and all-important choice to focus her energies on learning to eat normally. She chose to hide her scale and set a goal to concentrate on normal eating habits (not weight loss) for one month. Once that choice was made, she worked hard at following some basic guidelines that naturally thin people follow. Here are some of the steps I shared with Karen. Dr. Richard Stuart, psychological director for Weight Watchers International, has developed some of these guidelines which have helped millions of people struggling with weight control.[3]

Schedule three meals a day at regular times. You can train yourself to think about food only at certain times of the day. When you're out of control, structured meals can help diminish that obsession because you have previously decided that you will only eat at mealtimes. This will help you limit what, when, and how much you eat. You might want to start the day by planning your meals. This will give you a sense of control and something objective to refer to if you start to feel panicky about your new eating behavior.

Many of my clients have found that the following suggestions have helped them.

- Eat your food only at the family meal table.
- Do not allow yourself to nibble before, during, or after meal preparation. Be-

fore you put your fingers in the food, mentally set a goal to eat only when the meal is fully prepared. Use self-talk to help: "I'll enjoy my meal so much because I'm not spoiling my appetite by snitching."

- Concentrate on really experiencing your food. Notice the textures and smells. This is much more satisfying than frantically shoveling into your mouth everything you can get your hands on.

- Eat slowly. Consciously make an effort to chew each bite. Put your fork down in between bites.

- Drink a full glass of water before every meal. This will help you knock off three of the eight prescribed glasses of water a day. It will also fill you up so that you won't be so easily tempted to get off your eating plan.

- At some point during your meal, pause. Put your fork down, listen to table conversation or to some music in the background. Then resume eating. This will help break the impulsiveness of eating.

- Tell yourself, "It's absolutely normal to feel full after a meal." Your belt will feel tighter after you've eaten. But don't panic—in a few hours you won't feel full anymore and your body will be well nourished.

Schedule your snacks as small meals and be precise in terms of when, what, and how much is eaten. You want to be free from being obsessed with food all day long. Large variations in your eating schedule will defeat your efforts to control your thoughts about food. Dr. Stuart says, "If freedom from persistent urges to eat is important to you, the effort necessary to retrain yourself to think of food only at the times that you choose will be a small price to pay. Once you have reconditioned yourself to think of food at certain times only, you can go back to a more natural flexibility."[4]

I would like to point out here that some recent research has found that the human body functions better on smaller and more frequent meals than on the traditional three. "Think of a bathtub with a one-inch drain. Add water at a slow enough rate and the tub will never overflow. Add water too quickly and you'll slosh around in the results. Your body works on very much the same principle. Four or five equally caloric meals will flow smoothly down the metabolic pipeline. Large meals will overflow—and the body stores overflow calories as fat."[5]

As you snack, remember that:

- When you want a snack, take it to the meal table, sit down, and eat it slowly as you would a meal.
- Forbid yourself to eat in the car, on the bus, in the bedroom or bathroom, on the run, etc. This will help condition your eating to meal times only.

Those who fail to plan, plan to fail! One of the best tools available to help your progress toward normal eating is a daily planner. It is an inexpensive way to help control what you eat and to bring order to your daily food consumption. A spiral notebook is a good place to keep a running record of your nutrition plan. Papers don't get lost and you'll be able to look back over previous days to see your progress.

The daily plan basically consists of two charts. The first, "Tomorrow's Battle Plan," lists what you plan to eat for your meals and snacks the next day as well as the number of calories for each meal and snack. My clients usually like to fill in this chart at a time in the day when they feel vulnerable and lack will power. Concentrating on a plan or success strategy helps them avoid temptation. The second chart, "Today's Success Strategy," is to be filled in as you follow through with your battle plan. It gives you the opportunity to see yourself winning. Each chart will take one page per day. (Samples of both charts have been included for your use at the back of the book.)

Alisha found that having a daily plan was a great help. Late afternoons were a particularly hard time for her to stay out of the refrigerator. Now she sits down with a cup of tea every day at four o'clock to record "Tomorrow's Battle Plan." It gets her successfully through her vulnerable time and gives her a vision for the next day's success.

When are your vulnerable times with food? If evenings are tough, perhaps you'll want to record your plans after dinner. Maybe the break time at work is hard for you because everyone else is having coffee and donuts. If this is the case, try writing your battle plans during your break. You'll be amazed how uninteresting those donuts will become. On the next page is an example of what "Today's Success Strategy" might look like.

You may be asking, "Why do I have to count calories?" We use calorie counting in order to help you control weight while you are eating healthfully. You will learn that you control what you eat. We also use calorie recording to help take the impulsiveness out of eating. When you record what you will eat and list the calories before you eat them, you are much more likely not to snitch, nibble, or go for more. If you have had problems with self-starvation, calorie recording will help you learn

DATE:

TODAY'S SUCCESS STRATEGY

	TIME	PLACE	FOOD EATEN	CALORIES	THOUGHTS & FEELINGS
Breakfast	8:00	kitchen table	2 eggs, soft boiled 1 toast w/w 1 t. butter 1 c. coffee, plain	160 100 40 0 Subtotal: 300	I'm ready to face the day. Work will be good today and I have good energy
snacks	10:00	desk/work	1 c. coffee	0	good
Lunch	12:30	restaurant	Green salad Muffin 1 T. Salad dressing	50 100 100 Subtotal: 250	I enjoyed lunch with Marge. Things going well at work. Looking forward to spending the evening at home with the family.
Dinner	6:00	Kitchen table	Spaghetti 1 c. 1 pc. garlic toast Salad w/1 T. dressing	300 150 150 Subtotal: 600	The kids had so much to tell us about school. I'm glad they have good teachers. Bill seems extra tired. That concerns me.

TOTAL 1150

how much you can eat to gain or maintain your weight. You no longer have to look at a piece of bread and panic. You can allot for it as part of your daily plan and enjoy every bite without feeling guilty.

If you feel as though it is too much work to make daily menus, you may find it helpful to incorporate the plans offered by Weight Watchers Programs or by professional dieticians. A nutritionist can explain a balanced approach to food combinations and offer assistance and resources on the caloric content of food items.

Yes, it does take time and some energy to plan. But the benefits of normal eating are worth it. Set a goal to invest yourself in planning to succeed. You really do have what it takes to say goodbye to your eating disorder. Remember, if you aim at nothing, you'll be sure to hit it! Normal eating habits won't happen overnight, but as you plan, set goals, and take it one day at a time, you will see success.

Don't set yourself up to binge by skipping scheduled meals. People who starve themselves all day set themselves up to binge in the late afternoon or evening. Psychologically, they feel cheated of the food they thought about through the day; physically, they are tired from the day's work and improper nutrition; and emotionally, they have no fight power. The result? Usually a full-blown binge. Dr. Stuart calls this a "psychological calorie deficit." This is why he emphasizes that it is critical for those with eating disorders to maintain their eating schedules—whether they feel like it or not. Learning a new pattern demands consistency.

Most people with eating disorders don't feel like eating according to a plan because they are so conditioned to inconsistent eating patterns. But when they make the choice to stick with the plan regardless of their feelings, they do learn to eat normally. Yes, for a time it feels uncomfortable, but one or two months of discomfort is a small price to pay for a lifetime of increased control and normalcy.

177

The Battle Can Be Won!

Create your meals using a great deal of variety. Variety can be a good safeguard against setting yourself up for cravings. When you deprive yourself of certain foods, you may end up feeling psychologically deprived. The best way to avoid this is to vary the foods you choose at each meal. Mix crunchy with mushy foods, chewy with soft foods, orange with green, red with yellow.

I realize that ripping up your "safe" and "non-safe" food list is about the last thing you want to do. Your "good and bad" foods may be deeply ingrained in you. But to move toward normal eating you must set aside rigid lists. One way to do this is to begin adding a new item to your safe food list each week. Maybe this week you want to add a potato or an ear of corn or a piece of bread. When you are deciding which item to add, you are in control. You need not be fearful. You can do it, one step at a time!

When Karen first started therapy, I had her write down her safe and nonsafe foods. This helped both of us get in touch with her usual food intake when she was in control, and also showed us the foods which usually triggered her binges. During the first weeks in therapy, her list looked like this:

SAFE FOODS

Coffee, tea	Oatmeal
Diet pop	Lettuce
Yogurt	Tomatoes
Celery	Cabbage
Carrots	Spinach
Strawberries	Green beans
Cottage cheese	Chicken and beef broth

NONSAFE FOODS

Ding-dongs	Potatoes
Twinkies	All meats
Chips	Hard cheese
Pretzels	All cereal
Peanuts	Milk
Cookies	Fruit pies
Ice cream	Candy
Donuts	Sandwiches
Doritos	Eggs
All bread	Butter, oils

Gradually, Karen began to add one item a week from her nonsafe list to her safe foods list. Since her diet was very low in protein, the first item she added was a glass of milk. The next week she decided to eat an egg for breakfast occasionally. The following week she added a piece of bread at lunch time. Each week, Karen continued to add one more item to her safe list. After several months, she could actually handle going to a friend's home for a full-course meal without panicking. She had learned that moderate amounts of any food wouldn't make her fat. By increasing her safe foods, she decreased her trigger foods and heightened her own peace of mind.

We have to face the fact that we live in a food-oriented culture. In light of this, variety is a must to move toward normalcy. Eventually you will be stuck in a situation where you will have no control over the food being served. Someday you will have to face breads, steak, pastas, and desserts. If all of these foods are nonsafe items on your list, you will probably panic, embarrassing yourself and offending those around you. However, if your acceptable food list is expanded, you're less likely to set yourself up for failure and more likely to stick with a normal eating program.

The Battle Can Be Won!

Why don't you take a moment and do the exercise Karen did during her first weeks in therapy. Write down your safe foods and your nonsafe foods. Then set a goal for this week. Pick one food from your nonsafe food list and add it to your safe food list. Remember, any food eaten in moderation will not make you fat. Take the risk and decide to move toward normal eating habits. You'll be glad you did!

Do not restrict your food intake to less than 1200 calories per day. One question I am frequently asked is "How many calories can I eat and not gain weight?" Usually I encourage people not to restrict their calories below 1200 per day, because if they do, they put their bodies into a starvation state, altering its chemistry and slowing down its metabolic rate. As a result, their body burns calories less efficiently.

USE TRICKS THAT "NORMAL" EATERS USE

As you work with your plans for freedom, it can be helpful to try some tricks that many weight control programs use with great success. New behaviors are learned and developed. They don't happen automatically, and normal eating patterns will come easier if you utilize some of the following tips.

- Set short-range goals and force yourself to think in the here and now. One reason many anorexics and bulimics give up trying to eat normally is that they think they have to handle everything all at once. They look at the huge mountain of the overall goal rather than only at the one step that needs to be taken at the present moment. Rather than being overwhelmed with thoughts of the entire week, concentrate on making it through the next hour or the next meal.

- Reward yourself when you stick to your battle plan. Susie came up with a great reward system. Every meal she stuck to her battle plan, she earned a credit. As the credits accumulated, she treated herself with rewards. Here are some of her ideas:

    3 credits—a diet pop

    6 credits—renting a video movie

    9 credits—an extra morning at the athletic club with the kids in the nursery

    12 credits—a day at the beach with Marty

    15 credits—sign up for oil painting class

    20 credits—a new accessory for my wardrobe

  Be sure that you do not use food as a reward. Some people use food such as candy bars or donuts as a present for accomplishing a difficult task. While you are trying to learn to eat normally, substitute other rewards (like a bubble bath or a favorite magazine or a new bottle of nail polish) in place of food.

- Remove binge foods from your house. What you don't have, you can't eat.

- If your family wants sweets, and you know it would upset the household to deprive them of desserts, keep these items out of sight or in containers that are out of easy reach.

- Don't go grocery shopping while you're hungry. Write out your shopping list according to your battle plans, and shop on

a full stomach. This will help you stay
away from high calorie "extras."

All of the above ideas serve one purpose: They
make it hard for you to fudge on your battle plans. Don't
allow yourself to be surrounded by stimuli that will pull
out the worst in you. Instead, surround yourself with
stimuli that will help you toward your goals. As you make
wise choices, you'll be able to stand tall with many others
and confidently say, "I used to have an eating disorder,
but that's a part of my past!"

WHAT ABOUT EXERCISE?

Physicians working with patients in healthy
weight control programs recommend that a regular
exercise program be maintained three or four times a
week because exercise increases metabolic rate, causing
calories to be burned more efficiently. But remember,
your goal in exercise is moderation. Abusive exercise or
"overdoing it" causes lean body muscle loss which is
dangerous to your health.

Research from the Harvard Medical School labo-
ratories shows weight loss can occur without a loss of
lean body mass when a balanced exercise program is followed along with a balanced diet. In a recent study,
people were randomly assigned to exercise and nonexercise groups. Both groups received the same number of
calories in a balanced diet each day. After seven weeks
the nonexercise group lost eighteen pounds—eleven
pounds of fat, but seven pounds of lean muscle tissue.
The exercise group lost twenty-three pounds of fat but
at the same time gained four pounds of lean muscle tissue, which led to an overall weight loss of nineteen
pounds.[6]

THE SET POINT THEORY

During the past few years there has been an increasing volume of articles and reviews discussing the

idea that each person is born with a set point, an ideal body weight innately determined. The set point is the weight at which a person is most physiologically comfortable. Notice I said *physiologically,* not emotionally or psychologically comfortable according to societal standards. There can be a big difference between these comfort zones. For example, one woman 5'7" tall may have a set point of 125 pounds, while another may have an optimal weight of 135 pounds.

Proponents of the set point theory say that your metabolic rate speeds up or slows down to keep you at your set point. When you reduce your caloric intake to lose weight, your metabolism slows down. So everything equalizes. You eat less, burn less, and therefore remain the same. Your body organizes itself to balance energy intake and output so that you'll remain at your optimal weight.

Some doctors say that as you increase your caloric intake, your metabolism may speed up. Through a mechanism that may include a type of excess-calorie-burning tissue called "brown fat," you burn more while eating more. Overpower this calorie-overflow system and you risk creeping obesity.[7]

The most effective weapon to lower a set point is a balanced, sustained exercise program. Most fitness specialists agree that in order to maintain weight control and optimal fitness, a person should exercise at least three times a week. In order to improve one's fitness level and lose weight, an exercise regimen of four or more days a week is suggested. As you raise your metabolism through exercise, you also increase your amount of muscle tissue and lower your level of body fat. Muscle tissue burns more calories than fat.

I take the time to elaborate the set point theory because so many men and women I talk with are constantly comparing themselves to other people and coming out on the bottom. Many times I've heard clients say, "I have a friend who is the same height as I am and she weighs ten pounds less and never works at it." Chances are that friend has a lower optimal weight. This can be a real source of encouragement when you understand that weight loss struggles are not necessarily caused by weaknesses in personality but rather by built-in body chemistry.

It also means it is very important to decide on a realistic body weight that is best for your body and for your personal optimal fitness. The Twiggy look is definitely not for most people. There are some people who are born with a genetic make-up which lends itself to natural thinness all through life. Our society would like to press us into that type of a mold, but the fact is, most people are just not built that way.

A BIBLICAL PERSPECTIVE ON FOOD

My clients frequently say, "I wish I could live without food. Why didn't God make us so that all we need is one pill a day for energy? Why did He even give us food and the capacity for being fat when He knew it would be such a problem to so many of us?"

First Corinthians 6:12 states, "I can do anything I want to if Christ has not said no, but some of these things aren't good for me. Even if I am allowed to do them, I'll refuse to if I think they might get such a grip on me that I can't easily stop when I want to. For instance, take the matter of eating. God has given us an appetite for food and stomachs to digest it. But that doesn't mean we should eat more than we need. Don't think of eating as important, because some day God will do away with both stomachs and food" (TLB). Food and figures are temporary in God's eyes. Paul was writing to people in an Epicurean society—much like people in our society. They lived to eat. God's original design is just the opposite. His plan for us is to eat to live.

Food is linked, throughout Scripture and in Jesus' ministry, with relaxed friendship. Christ and His followers reclined at the food table and probably told stories for hours. Food was present, but it was not the center of attention. It was simply available for nourishment, enjoyment, and as a reminder of God's covenant to provide for His children. Man's twisted thinking sometimes makes food the center of attention rather than fellowship and people. Food as a compulsive focus or a mental obsession is a perverted delusion of what God meant it to be. God always prefers that we emphasize people and relationships more than substances and things. When we warp God's design with twisted thinking about food, eating disorders can take hold.

A SUCCESS STORY

Let me finish this chapter by filling you in on Karen's success. After one month of following the guidelines we established, Karen's weight remained the same, but her energy level and peace of mind increased.

"The first two weeks were really hard. There were days when I desperately wanted to skip meals and drink diet Coke. There were evenings I felt like I was on the very edge of going back to those gross gorging sessions. Usually at times like that I asked Dan (her husband) or Carla (her close friend) to pray with me for strength to keep with the program.

"After two weeks, the fight seemed to lessen. I guess the reconditioning process had begun to take effect. After one month of forcing myself to stick with the guidelines, I actually began to believe that I could eat like a normal person. The cravings to binge and purge came only once in a while instead of several times a day. The desire to starve decreased even faster because I had so much more energy than before. Life really was more enjoyable. Colors began to look more brilliant, the sun shone brighter, music sounded clearer, and my family even noticed I was smiling and laughing again.

"It has now been five months since I made the choice to hang up my scale and to focus wholeheartedly on eating healthily. Believe it or not, I now eat 1600 calories a day, as opposed to my former 600-700 calories a day. Starving, bingeing, and purging are no longer a part of my life. Instead, I exercise forty-five minutes three days a week to keep my metabolic rate up so my body will efficiently utilize the food I eat. Sometimes I have the temptation to purge or to skip meals when I feel like I've eaten too much, but I know this would only slow down my metabolism and work against me. So I force myself to stick with the program.

"One of the nice things about learning to eat normally is that I really enjoy food now instead of being paranoid about it. I'm actually tasting and enjoying each delicious bite. On top of that I now weigh two pounds less than I did five months ago. I've gained three pounds of lean muscle tissue and have lost several inches as a result of exercising. Though it was hard and scary getting started, I'll never be sorry for choosing to learn how to eat normally. After experiencing this new lease on life, I never want to go back to the bondage I was in before . . . and since I'm taking responsibility for what goes in and out of my mouth, I know I never will!"

Let me encourage you to work with a nutritionist and a counselor who can help you establish normal eating habits and find the optimal weight for your body. Part of your unique design may include a set point. This will no doubt be different from the ideal weight that television and fashion magazines give you. You may have to come to grips with the fact that you were not meant to wear a size five. This is part of the healing process. You will be miserable if you try to fight your original design the rest of your life. But as you learn and discover more about your body and accept the way you were created, you can move from a stance of apathetic existing to celebrated living!

CHAPTER 11, NOTES

1. Bob Schwartz, *Diets Don't Work* (Galveston, Tex.: Breakthru Publishing, 1982).

2. Peter Nash, M. D., "A Matter of Fat," *Shape* (March 1985), p. 142.

3. Richard Stuart, *Act Thin, Stay Thin* (New York: W. W. Norton, 1979).

4. Ibid.

5. Irving Dardik and Denis Waitley, *Quantum Fitness* (New York: Pocket Books, 1984), p. 56.

6. Nash, "A Matter of Fat."

7. Dardik and Waitley, *Quantum Fitness.*

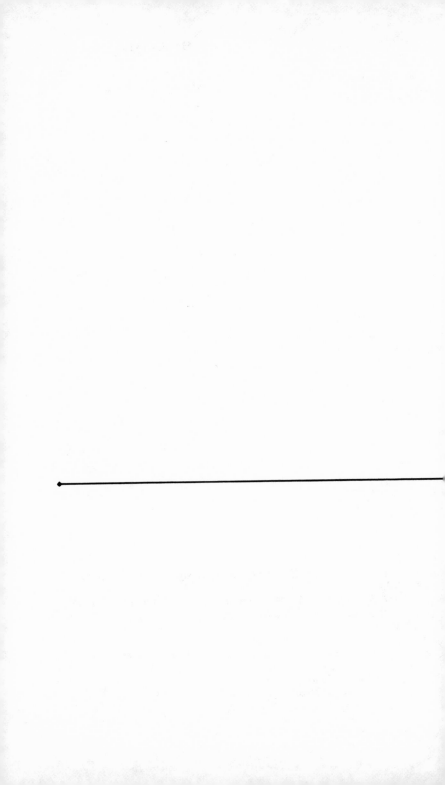

ALTERNATIVES
LEAD TO FREEDOM

The growth and support group was about to begin. Men, women, and teenagers gathered in a crowded conference room to learn about themselves and eating disorders. A contagious type of hope filled the room. I prayed, "Oh, God, please help these precious people learn to grow and experience new freedom tonight."

We had been meeting consistently for many months. Tonight we were going to discuss alternatives that lead to freedom from being obsessed by food. This group wasn't full of rookies. They had already dismissed the misconception that someone, somewhere, had a pat answer and an instant cure for their problem. Instead, they had decided to face the facts. They had chosen to dismantle, with God's help, the imprisoning walls around them one brick at a time.

The sound of crinkling papers filled the room as each person pulled out their homework assignment, "Tools That Help Me Stay Out of My Prison." Conversation began, and for the next one and a half hours they talked while I listened.

This chapter represents a list of healthy choices that my clients have found helpful. The tools that are offered and stories that are told are dedicated to you from people who have made tremendous strides toward freedom. If they could meet you in person, they would encourage you to aggressively grab on to the keys that have helped unlock their prison doors. They would say to you, "Don't give up. Your freedom is worth fighting for. If we can do it, you can do it!"

GET HELP

First on almost everybody's list was to *get help from someone trained in the area of eating disorders.* You've heard me stress this before, but it is so important I want to say it again. It is virtually impossible to overcome an eating disorder without the help of a professional.

You may be thinking, "But I can't let anyone find out about this. Who knows what they will think." Counselors who are knowledgeable about eating disorders understand what contributes to your problem and are in a position to compassionately help you. They are also required by law to keep everything you disclose strictly confidential unless you give them permission to do otherwise. With professional help, you are guaranteed absolute privacy. No one will find out about your problem unless you tell them yourself.

People often have the idea that only severely mentally disturbed people visit counselors. This is a major misconception, especially in many religious circles. A counselor is simply someone who offers consultation based on his or her expertise in understanding the human mind and behavior. Many people talk with counselors simply for personal growth and development. Talking with a counselor about your problems can be a very positive experience.

If you're feeling apprehensive about seeking help, you are not alone. Just about every client I have talked with about anorexia or bulimia has experienced similar fears.

Susan shared her feelings of apprehension with the rest of the group: "I remember how fearful I was to call for an appointment. I thought that only really sick people talked to therapists. I was ashamed that God and I couldn't work this out alone. I figured if I was spiritual enough, I wouldn't have this problem. I was scared to death Mike [her husband] would find out, and I was convinced he would divorce me if he knew I vomited and took huge doses of laxatives. [Mike was sitting next to her in the circle.]

"It has been over five months since I made that first phone call, and I'm so glad I did something right for a change. I've become a different person since I started counseling. I know I have a lot more to learn, but it's so fulfilling to see how much progress I've made. It's good to know I'm not alone and that there are answers and there really is hope."

God often uses other people to help us out of tight spots. It isn't unspiritual to ask for help. Proverbs 1:5 says, "A wise man will hear and increase in learning, and a man of understanding will acquire wise counsel" (NASB). Reach out and get the support you need. You are worth it.

RELEASE CREATIVE ENERGIES OUTSIDE THE KITCHEN

Many struggling with anorexia and bulimia spend hours in the kitchen creating lavish gourmet meals and fancy desserts. The anorexic will cook and then watch everyone else eat. The bulimic will usually eat with the rest of the family and then purge. Either way, this type of activity only serves to keep those with eating disorders obsessed with food. It does nothing to aid recovery.

This doesn't mean you have to give up creative cooking the rest of your life. However, when you're trying to get an eating disorder under control, it's best not to set yourself up for failure by focusing excess energies on food, especially your favorite foods. As you gain good coping skills and make steps in recovery, creative cooking will become less of an anxious obsession and more of a relaxing joy.

FLEE THE SCENE OF THE CRIME

When the cravings start to churn and you feel like you're moving into five-speed overdrive toward the kitchen, flee the scene of the crime. It may sound ridiculous, but sometimes the best way to handle a craving for food is to run the other direction.

Mary Lou shared a story with me during a counseling session that I'll never forget. "I had been doing well—I had not skipped a meal for four days. [This was great progress because she had been eating only one small meal a day for three years.] It was Saturday, and we finished lunch and were relaxing in the living room. Suddenly I got the biggest urge to take a box of laxatives. [Mary Lou used starvation, laxatives, and purging.] I battled the thoughts back and forth in my mind for twenty minutes. Finally, I was sick of hassling it all, and walked up the stairs to the main level of my home to get some food from the cupboard. I was angry and anxious; I hated myself for wanting to blow it, but I also hated feeling full and fat.

"I got to the top of the stairs, saw the front door, and made a mad dash outside. I ran around the neighborhood for the next twenty minutes. I'm not a jogger, so that was a major run for me. I ran and cried and prayed and ran and cried and prayed some more. The battle inside me was exasperating. When I walked back into the house, I was different. I had won that battle. I had no desire to take the laxatives and knew I would be able to face dinner. It helped to literally flee temptation. By leaving, I gave myself a chance to talk to God and to get His help. He gave me the added strength I needed to be a winner."

SEE YOURSELF WINNING

One of the things I enjoy doing with my clients is helping them use their imagination for condemnation-free living. Use of the imagination for weight control has been shown to be very effective in predicting the long-term maintenance of weight loss. Dieters who imagine themselves as successful are more likely to maintain their weight control.[1]

God in His wisdom not only tells us to use our imaginations for good, but He also tells us what to do with unhealthy imaginings. Second Corinthians 10:4-5 says, "Destroy speculations and every lofty thing raised up against the knowledge of God." In other words, God tells us to cancel out bad imaginings that are contrary to

The Battle Can Be Won!

His truths. He tells us to do away with thoughts that defeat and condemn us because "as a man thinks in his heart, so is he" (Proverbs 23:7 KJV). Here are some examples of a bulimic and an anorexic who were able to win their battles by taking their thoughts captive and being creative with their imaginations.

A BULIMIC WHO SAW HERSELF WINNING . . . WON!

Debra came for her regular weekly session, and I could tell that she was highly agitated and didn't feel like talking. I soon found out that she had experienced a terrible conflict at work and had spent the last thirty minutes outside my office writing out a junk food grocery list. She planned to stop at the store on the way home from counseling to stock up for her evening binge. All afternoon she had daydreamed about what she would buy and how she would eat it. She looked me square in the eye and said, "Don't try to talk me out of it. I've been planning this all day, and there's no way I can stop it now."

I suggested she try to use her imagination in a constructive and creative way. I asked her to sit back in her chair, close her eyes, and then I helped her unwind with some relaxation techniques. When she was relaxed, I then proceeded to help her use her imagination to see herself succeeding rather than failing. I said something like this:

"Debra, I want you to picture yourself with a big smile on your face. If you have trouble visualizing this, think back to one of your favorite snapshots where your smile was big and bright. Your head is high, your shoulders are back, and you exude confidence. Everything about you communicates strength and stability. You feel great.

"As you leave the counseling session tonight to drive home, you notice on the seat beside you the grocery list you made for your binge. You come to a red light, look at the list, pick it up, tear it into a hundred tiny pieces, and say out loud, 'Bingeing is stupid. I don't want that junk shoveled into my mouth.' The light turns green and you toss the pieces of paper in the trash bag.

"Five minutes later you approach the grocery store where you normally shop for a binge. You look at the store and a huge smile covers your face as you drive by it. With confidence in your voice you say, 'Good job, Debra! Now you're thinking smart. You don't need to binge. Tonight will be a good night, and tomorrow morning will be better when you wake up without a sugar hangover and with lots of energy.'

"Now picture yourself walking in the front door and greeting your family with a contented heart and peace of mind. You walk in the kitchen and prepare the family meal, placing just enough on your plate to satisfy your hunger. You eat your meal and clean up the kitchen without eating any extra scraps or leftovers. By now it's 8:00 P.M. and you decide to tackle one of the items on your 'To Do' list. See yourself doing that task. When the task is complete you feel satisfied, peaceful, and fulfilled because you have accomplished one of your goals.

"During the rest of the evening you feel pleasantly relaxed. As you lay your head down on your pillow and turn off the light, you breathe a deep sigh of relief and thank God for another day of victory. And then you begin to talk to Him about some of the deep things in your heart. Go ahead and talk with Him right now."

When Debra finished praying, she blurted out, "I can't believe this. I planned a huge binge all day long, and now I have absolutely no desire to do it." Debra had pictured herself failing all day. She had set herself up for failure by imagining herself failing. During our session together these thoughts were combated and reversed. For the first time she saw herself victorious over a binge.

The next day she called me. "I can't tell you how excited I am. I had no desire to binge all night. I had a beautiful evening with my family instead of being self-absorbed with my bag of food."

AN ANOREXIC WHO SAW HERSELF WINNING . . . WON!

Perhaps you don't battle with bingeing and purging. Perhaps your difficulties come when you have to eat even tiny portions of low-calorie food. Martha shared your same struggle. She wanted to eat normally, but was intensely fearful of gaining weight.

Through our therapy sessions Martha began to learn that she had the tremendous power of choice. She could choose what to allow her mind to imagine. She learned that some imaginations were harmful and others were helpful in recovering from anorexia. She shared one of her most effective imagery tools with me in a letter she wrote while on vacation.

> Dear Pam,
>
> You might like to know that I have successfully been eating three times a day while here in California. Whenever it is time to eat a meal, my first response is to skip it. All the patterns of the past flood in at that point. But I began to use imagery before meals and it has really helped. One thing I do is picture the devil standing in front of me as I approach the meal time. He is cocky and laughing mockingly at me. He cackles loudly, saying, "You're gonna die! Ha! Ha! You're gonna die from starvation! You'll never get well! Ha! Ha! I've got you now!" I picture him big, black, and reeking with the stench of death. Then I picture myself looking him straight in the face, saying, "The joke's on you, buster! I'm going to eat. I'm in charge here, and Jesus and I are the victors." As I say *Jesus*, he always shrinks to the

size of a rat and scurries down a little black hole as fast as he can.

You might think this is a little far-fetched, but it really works for me. I'm working on creating another imagery tool this week. I want to make the most of a good thing. See you next week.

Love,
Martha

Martha's imagination is certainly vivid. The imagery she used is also based on teachings from Scripture. James 4:9 says, "Submit . . . to God. Resist the devil and he will flee from you." Martha pictured herself submitting to God (by choosing to do what He wanted her to do for good health) and resisting the devil (by telling him that she and Jesus were in charge, not he).

Be inventive and picture yourself succeeding in areas where you usually fail. It might seem awkward at first. This is because you have rehearsed failing in your mind for so long. It's a challenge to switch gears, but not impossible. You have the power and privilege of this choice. Use it—for your own good.

THROW OUT YOUR SCALE

Many of my clients have thrown out their scales because it had become one of the strongest forces influencing their continued obsession with food and weight. This may be true for you, too. When a person steps on a scale, one of three things will occur: the scale will show you have gained, maintained, or lost weight.

If the scale shows you have gained weight since the last time you weighed, you will probably feel defeated because your discipline doesn't seem to be paying off.

Terry told me of her exasperation when she stepped on the scale: "I couldn't believe it. I had not binged for three days. I was sure I'd weigh less, but the scale showed I had gained two pounds. I was so bummed out I said, 'Why try?' and spent the next two hours binge-ing."

Lydia shares a similar story: "I had starved all day and decided to **weigh** before I went to bed. I had already planned to eat three small meals the next day, but that idea fell apart when I got on the scale. I had gained a pound. That really depressed me, so I didn't eat any-thing for the next two days. I was working at getting well and eating healthy foods, but when I saw the weight on the scale, I panicked."

If the scale shows you weigh the same as the last time you weighed, you'll be disappointed.

Cathy said, "For five days I ate small amounts three times a day. I didn't skip one meal. This helped me not want to binge. I made it all week. I stepped on the scale and couldn't believe my weight didn't drop—not even one pound. It makes me wonder if all this healthy eating is really worth it."

Even when the scale shows you have lost weight, it can work against you.

"It had been four months since I was released from the hospital," Miriam told me. "When I got home, I promised myself I wouldn't use the scale I had hidden under my bed. Last week I got curious about my weight and decided to weigh just once. The scale read 100 pounds. Then I got to thinking, 'I'll bet I can make it read 99 tomorrow.' So I skipped two meals. When I got on the scale in the morning, I weighed 99 pounds. That started the ball rolling; I was 'high' on losing weight again." Two weeks later, Miriam's doctor placed her back in the hospital again for tube feedings. Her scale was her enemy.

Wendy's story shows how weight loss can work against anyone struggling with bulimia.

"I got on the scale and had lost two pounds. I was elated! That night I went with friends to the movies and out for pizza, which is usually one of my binge trigger foods. I figured I was safe since I had lost two pounds. But one piece of pizza led to seven, and by then I had lost control. After two weeks of no bingeing, I blew it. I would have been better off not weighing!"

Your scale is your enemy. Do you want to get your eating under control? If you do, throw out your scale. It caters to distorted thinking about food. First, learn how to eat normally and think healthy. Then, if need be, deal with weight loss once you've stabilized a normal, healthy eating pattern.

DEVISE OPPORTUNITIES TO WIN DURING YOUR VULNERABLE TIMES

Everybody has weaknesses and areas of vulnerability. One of the keys to staying out of food's imprisonment is to know when you are most likely to be weak and then plan around it. No soldier goes to the battle front without a well-planned strategy. If free time is a battle, plan a strategy to be a winner. Here are some ideas others have used.

Keep tempting things out of sight. Melanie: "I'm most vulnerable during my break at work. Our eating room is loaded with food machines. Now I pack a healthy lunch in the morning— when I am strong—and stay out of the machine room. If I don't see it, I don't want it."

Set short-term goals and plan rewards for yourself. Katy: "My vulnerable time is driving to and from work. I used to hit all of the fast food restaurants in one area each trip. Now I have a specific plan for that weakness. Before I leave in the morning I eat a small but healthy breakfast. Then I tell myself, 'Your only goal for this next hour is to drive straight to work with no stops.' I leave the checkbook at home and take just enough change to buy a soda with my lunch. Then I pray and sing all the way to work."

Tony: "Weekends used to be my bummer days. Now they're fun. I reward myself on Saturday for all the binges I passed up during the week. I use my calculator to determine how much money I've saved through the week when I turned down a binge in the heat of temptation. Then I go buy a new pair of earrings or something special for myself. Sometimes Martin and I will use the money to go to the movies or to buy records. This reward system really keeps me motivated through the week, and it gives me something fun to do on weekends."

Plan your meal times. Patty: "Church potlucks are my weakness. As a pastor's wife, I'm faced with them continually. I've learned to see potlucks as an opportunity to win. Now I take two dishes that my family enjoys and that I know won't trigger a binge. Once all the food is on the table, I look to see what I can handle and what would set me off. With this plan of action, I'm much more relaxed and can enjoy the people rather than being paranoid about the food."

Marcia: "Any mealtime used to scare me to death. I didn't want to eat anything for fear of gaining weight. Now I have a plan. I know exactly how many calories I can allot for each meal to maintain my healthy post-anorexic weight. I stick to these planned food courses and tell myself, 'You don't have to be afraid. This food will nourish your body and you won't gain weight. You know exactly how many calories you're eating, so enjoy the food and relax.' Working with my counselor on setting up a three-meal-a-day plan really helped take the fear out of eating for me."

Plan your free times. Marty: "Evenings are tough for me. I'm busy at work all day and have no desire to binge, but when I get home I'm keyed up, and food relaxes me and brings consolation. At least I used to think it did. Actually I ended up with more anxiety, hating myself after eating so much. Now I plan my evenings. Every morning I have a fifteen-minute break at work. That's my time to plan a strategy for that evening. Some of the things I do that have helped are:

- take a bubble bath and read one of my favorite magazines
- watch TV with a project that will keep my hands busy, such as crafts, sewing, needlepoint, laundry, or ironing
- write letters
- clean closets, organize my desk, redo files
- go to the movies with friends
- go shopping or browse in bookstores
- exercise at the health spa or with a record album on aerobics
- ask a friend to go out for coffee
- listen to my relaxation tape or other favorite tapes
- read a favorite book
- ride my exercise bike during the evening news
- take my dog for a leisurely walk in the park
- pamper myself with a facial or manicure"

Enlist the help of your friends. Tarah: "My weakness is the goodies at work. People are always bringing donuts, cookies, and munchies to eat during staff meetings. I used to dread those times. Now everyone knows not to offer them to me. Three months ago, I told them I would appreciate it if they didn't offer me the goodies. I explained I had set some goals for weight control, and asked if they would support me by not offering me snacks. Everyone was very understanding and they really have been helpful. It was scary for me to be honest and to ask for their help, but now I can enjoy staff meetings."

Make positive statements of truth. Sandy: "Often vulnerable times hit me when I least expect it. One thing that really helps is to pull out a 3x5 card I carry with me in my purse. Side one says: "Stop! And think!" Side two says: "You are making fantastic progress. Remember how far you have come. You don't want to give in now. God is with you. You can do all things through Christ who strengthens you. God is providing a way of escape for you right now. See it and grab it.""

Write in a journal. Tracy: "Whenever I hit weak times in the day and feel that driven urge to starve or to binge, I write in my journal. I'm not used to honestly expressing myself to others. Writing in a journal gives me a chance to face my deep-down feelings and to discover why I feel as I do. It's safe to explore myself on paper because the pages can't talk back. This gives me an opportunity to win, because each time I write, I learn more about what makes me tick—and that's progress!"

Arrange your schedule to avoid being overwhelmed. Linda: "In the morning I get up and feel overwhelmed with everything that needs to be done. I panic, which leads me to the refrigerator. Now I have a plan of action and turn my mornings into an opportunity to win. I set my alarm fifteen minutes earlier and sit at the kitchen table with a cup of coffee and my daily planner. On the left side of the page I write down the things that need to be done in order of priority. Then on the right I try to plan exactly what jobs I'll do for the day and what can be left for another day. Writing out a planned list takes away the confusion in doing my responsibilities. As I get each job done, I take a big red marker and cross another accomplishment off the list. I gain great satisfaction from seeing my progress through the day."

It is important to remember that starving, bingeing, and purging are learned behaviors. Learned behavior can be changed and another behavior substituted for it. Your behavior can change as you take personal responsibility to learn how to change. In this chapter I've described some of the tools others have successfully used to bring about change. Let me encourage you to step out and apply them. Take a risk toward good health. Yes, you will make mistakes, but so does everyone else. Try to see a mistake as an opportunity to learn. It's from blunders that we grow and develop and become all God wants us to be. Don't limit yourself from reaching your full potential. "Be strong and courageous. Do not be afraid or terrified . . . for the LORD your God goes with you; he will never leave you nor forsake you" (Deuteronomy 31:6).

CHAPTER 12, NOTES

1. Richard Stuart, "Weight Loss and Beyond: Are They Taking It Off and Keeping It Off?" *Behavioral Medicine* (1980): 151-194.

A WORD TO LOVED ONES

As the small groups at the seminar began interacting, I noticed one family of three just to my right. The daughter sat between her parents, and it was obvious that she was being put on the spot. The seven members of the group were peering at her while her mom and dad commented about her in exasperation. I could tell her parents were angry, confused, and torn up inside. Sandy was on edge, defensive, and becoming very skilled at blocking out the complaints and frustrations they voiced. Their family, which formerly had experienced a love and closeness, was being destroyed because of Sandy's anorexia.

Unfortunately, anorexia nervosa and bulimia affect more people than the person obsessed with food. As the defying grip of an eating disorder clamps deeper onto a person's lifestyle, loved ones suffer, too. Because the anorexic or bulimic feels isolated or rejected, communication can be difficult. Since many anorexics and bulimics refuse to admit they have a problem, those who care often feel shoved aside and confused.

In this chapter I'd like to discuss how you can help a person struggling with an eating disorder. The guidelines offered are those I share in family therapy. If you are feeling helpless and overwhelmed by what is happening in your relationship with a victim, my prayer is that you will receive encouragement and wisdom from the pages that follow. Let's first discuss a few things you should not do.

RESPONSES YOU NEED TO AVOID

Don't get into power struggles over food. The anorexic or bulimic is an expert at controlling her food intake. When you interfere and try to take control, beware. Don't attempt to cram food into the anorexic—you'll simply anger her. Don't try to forcefully stop the bulimic from bingeing or purging—unless you have been asked to do so. Some bulimics do ask family members to physically remove them from the binge site if they feel like they're going to lose control. This is fine, but only when it is agreed on beforehand.

Leave advice about meal and food planning in a counselor's hands. Any professional who is competent in helping the eating disordered will not let these issues slide. In fact, many counselors work closely with nutrition experts who can help the eating disordered learn exactly what their body needs in order to lose, gain, or maintain weight.

Don't offer pat answers. Anorexics and bulimics often complain that family members don't understand and always offer pat answers. I've made a list of some of the most common platitudes that are offered. These usually drive away those who are struggling.

- "Just start eating and be normal like everyone else."
- "I've never had a weight problem. I've eaten three meals a day all my life. Why don't you do what I do?"
- "Just pray about it and trust the Lord."
- "Can't you see what you're doing to yourself? You've got to stop this and stop it now!"
- "If your friends are making it hard for you to recover from your eating disorder, go find some new ones."
- "You should read your Bible more."
- "Pull yourself together and get on with life!"
- "Once you get right with God, you'll be fine."

Proverbs 15:23 says, "A man finds joy in giving an apt reply—and how good is a timely word!" Pat answers are rarely timely words. But as you ask God for insight,

He will help you find words that will bring encouragement to the eating disordered.

Don't impose guilt. Proverbs 12:18 says, "Reckless words pierce like a sword, but the tongue of the wise brings healing." When you are worn out from helping, it's easy to make offhand remarks. Usually they involve blaming the anorexic or bulimic for the misery of the rest of the family. Comments frequently heard are, "You're ruining our family!" or "Nothing is the same since you started this crazy behavior!" or "It sure would be nice to have things at home the way they used to be." These remarks do not motivate the eating disordered to change their behavior. They may, however, drive them into deeper isolation and despair.

Don't blame yourself. I remember talking with the mother of an anorexic who was convinced that her daughter's disorder was entirely her fault. She was guilt-ridden and continually blamed herself for everything she hadn't done to be a better mother.

One of the things I stress in family therapy is that an eating disorder is not any one person's fault. Moms and dads do not cause eating disorders. Spouses and loved ones cannot make anyone anorexic or bulimic. Depending on how they choose to relate to the eating disordered, family members can enhance or inhibit the recovery process, but they cannot be the sole cause of the problem.

Let me encourage you to treat yourself with dignity, even when it seems like things in your family aren't going well. You will have ups and downs. In the midst of your hardships, try not to be hard on yourself. Try to realize you are doing the best you can.

WHAT SHOULD YOU DO?

Lovingly confront an anorexic or bulimic with her symptoms. Left untreated, an eating disorder can become deeply ingrained in a person's lifestyle. It may be fatal. If you detect the symptoms of anorexia or bulimia in a loved one, loving confrontation is a must.

I've talked with many anorexics and bulimics who desperately wanted someone to notice their peculiar patterns. Some go so far as to leave vomit in the toilet or diet pills on the counter. Be aware of ways your loved one may be crying out for your help. They may want you to intervene.

Even if you feel that they have attempted to hide all the evidence of their disorder, talk to them about it. Take the risk of mentioning that you have noticed specific signs and symptoms in their behavior that are characteristic of anorexia or bulimia. You will be throwing them a life line—whether they realize it or not. A negative reaction from your loved one may be uncomfortable for you, but it won't be harmful. The avoidance of confrontation, however, can ruin a relationship and a life.

Get professional help for family members under legal age. Prior to the legal age of adulthood, parents are responsible for the welfare of their children. Your child may kick, scream, and threaten to hate you for life when you first mention the idea of counseling, but you will be doing them a great disservice if you don't require them to get help. It's never too early to confront the issue, but it can be too late. Acting quickly can save a life.

I would also encourage you to do all you can to help your family member get into a support group in addition to professional, one-on-one counseling. Research shows that the most important feature of a support group is the experience of sharing fears and misery and positive progress with others who "really know what it's all about."[1]

Get support for yourself. You are not the only person who is seeking to encourage and care for someone with an eating disorder. And there is no reason for you to experience this challenge alone. Many family members have received support from their pastors, Bible study groups, Overeaters Anonymous organizations, professional counselors, and close friends in whom they can confide. Remember, we are built with a need to be interdependent with others. Paul tells us that as Christian individuals we are to see ourselves collectively as Christ's body. He exhorts believers, saying, "There should be no division in the body, but that its parts should have equal concern for each other. If one part suffers, every part suffers with it; if one part is honored, every part rejoices with it" (1 Corinthians 12:25-26). A support system can help buffer the storms and heighten the joy of victories.

In recent years numerous organizations have been formed which offer support to eating disorder victims and their loved ones. I encourage you to write to the organizations listed in the back of this book. They can give you more information about the growth and support groups in your city. Many of them also offer a regular newsletter that can give you a good source of information for learning about eating disorders and how to relate to those who struggle with them.

Find out as much as you can about eating disorders. A great deal of anxiety can be reduced when you gather facts and begin to understand the behavioral and emotional patterns of the eating disordered. Read books and articles; attend seminars on anorexia and bulimia. Find out what current research is uncovering. The more you understand what contributes to your loved one's eating disorder, the easier it will be for you to detect the dynamics of your strained relationship. Find out if there are any changes *you* can make that will help, rather than expecting them to do all the changing.

Margie, the mother of an anorexic, learned that common family dynamics are sometimes found among those with eating disorders. These families often place more importance on loyalty and closeness than on autonomy and self-realization. Many times the parents are overprotective, and consequently the child's independence is curtailed. As a result, these children have difficulty seeing themselves as individuals separate from their parents or family.[2]

Another pattern seen in these families is that there is a rigid line drawn between the family and the outside world. Whenever one family member is involved in some activity, the rest of the family gets involved. This tends to leave the child with the idea that the family is safe, but the outside world is dangerous.[3]

Not all of these characteristics are found in all families, but a couple of the dynamics that Margie was made aware of were a part of their family experience. By recognizing her overprotectiveness through her research of the problem, she was in a position to begin to change. In the months that followed, she devised ways to allow her daughter to express more independence and autonomy. The exciting byproduct from all of this was that their relationship was less strained and much happier. Margie's research paid off.

Require the eating disordered to take responsibility for her actions. In other words, make your loved one accountable for her behavior. You may need to put a lock on the refrigerator, take the lock off the bathroom door, hide the scales, or require her to buy her own ritual foods. The last thing you want to do is to reinforce her destructive behavior by allowing her to shirk her responsibility to the rest of the family. I've seen some bulimics put families in debt while spending over $200 a week on binge food. I've seen families restricted from enjoying certain restaurants simply because a salad bar wasn't available for their anorexic child. Don't allow one person to manipulate the activities of your family.

Get in touch with your feelings. Very often family members ignore, deny, or swallow their anger, frustration, and fears. They hope that in time everything will pass and be all right. When I see denial and avoidance happening in a family, I point out that this is detrimental to everyone involved. You can pretend you don't have cancer, but that cancer will still eat away at you if left untreated. The best thing to do is to acknowledge that you have strong feelings and deal with them openly and honestly.

It may be helpful for you to keep a record of your emotions by jotting them down in a journal or a spiral notebook. Sometimes seeing what you feel in black and white can help you clarify and understand your feelings. Seek to understand yourself and the ways you respond emotionally. This growth process can benefit you and your family members, too.

Talk openly and honestly about your feelings. I've found that those with eating disorders are highly perceptive of the nonverbal cues people give them. This is why transparency on your part is so important. Talk about your feelings openly. This will help the eating disordered know where you stand and get rid of any unhealthy guessing games.

Those in bondage to an eating disorder often alienate the people who love them most. The anorexic and bulimic need people surrounding them who will remain open, even in the heat of a struggle. Work hard at expressing yourself truthfully and showing honest care and concern. In doing so you'll provide a healing arena in which your loved one can experience new dimensions of wholeness.

Be honest with an anorexic or bulimic about her appearance. If she has gained weight, an anorexic needs to hear the reality that she is becoming more beautiful. On the other hand, the ninety-pound anorexic who looks like she's just stepped out of a concentration camp needs to hear that she looks emaciated. She sees her thinness as beautiful, and if her perception of reality isn't challenged, she may starve herself into the grave. Bulimics need to hear that their swollen glands or puffy, blood-shot eyes are not attractive.

Attitude, tone of voice, and timing are critical factors in confrontation. Remember, the Bible says "speak the truth in love," not just "speak the truth." If you can't say it in a loving way, it's best not to say it at all.

Talk about issues other than food. Those with eating disorders are obsessed with thoughts of food. When family members have frequent discussions about dieting, thinness, and physical appearances, this adds to the victim's obsessions. You can help the eating disordered by avoiding comments about your own weight, such as, "I just have to take off five pounds!" or "My thighs are too fat." Instead, focus your discussions away from the physical externals and move them toward internal character qualities. Let them hear that you appreciate their kindness, patience, or enthusiasm. Tell them what you like about the person they are on the inside.

It is also helpful to take special care in giving attention to their personal interests. If they find computers, music, Bible study, or mystery books appealing, do what you can to cultivate and support their development in those areas. Any time spent absorbed in these interests means less time spent obsessed by food.

Listen. One of the greatest gifts you can give your loved one is listening to them. Listening communicates genuine caring and will gain trust. I've heard it said that the average time parents spend listening and actively communicating with their children is three minutes a day. Most of us are quick to give opinions and advice. The anorexic and bulimic are likely to know more about their problem than you do. What they really need is someone with whom they can feel safe to share transparently.

Show love and affection. There will be many times in the recovery process when the eating disordered in your family will seem unlovely. Fits of rage aren't pretty. Depression is unbecoming. When we see these reactions, we naturally withdraw love and affection. But it's in these rough points that love and affection continue to be needed. Rage, anger, and isolation are catalyzed by deep hurts and confusion. Those hurts need to be healed, and the best healing balm I know is unconditional love.

Hang in there! No doubt you have wanted to throw in the towel. You are not alone. Healing takes time, and growth toward wholeness is a process of advances and setbacks. There will be times you'll feel you don't care and want to give up. When a setback occurs, don't be devastated by thinking that all is lost. It's not. This is just part of the growth process.

There have been a few times as a counselor that I have felt like giving up on a client. I'm not proud to say that, but it is the truth. When I get to that last strained point and my inner resources for giving are drained, I know that it is time for me to spend time with the Source of all strength and healing. It's during those times that I cry out for discernment and wisdom. I ask God for renewed strength and energy so that I can give beyond my own reserves.

It's wonderful to know that God has not called you to give only out of your own strength. He will use your strength and at the same time supply you with resources beyond your abilities. He has promised to give to you all the love and energy you need to keep going: "And my God will meet all your needs according to his glorious riches [not your limited resources] in Christ Jesus" (Philippians 4:19). When you feel like giving up, let me encourage you to heed the words of Jesus when He says, "Come to me, all you who are weary and burdened, and I will give you rest" (Matthew 11:28).

CHAPTER 13, NOTES

1. G. Lenihan and C. Sanders, "Guidelines for Group Therapy with Eating Disorder Victims," *Journal of Counseling and Development* 63 (December 1984): 252-254.

2. Salvador Minuchin, *Psychosomatic Families: Anorexia Nervosa in Context* (Cambridge, Mass.: Harvard Press, 1978).

3. Kim Lampson, eating disorders seminar, Providence Medical Center, Seattle, Washington, May 13-14, 1983.

HEALING
IS AVAILABLE

"I always wanted to be healed so I'd never have to struggle with eating again. When I first became a Christian, I was sure God would deliver me. My spiritual conversion was total. I stopped smoking and drinking immediately, and everything else in my life seemed to fall into place." Danielle was explaining her history of bulimia to me.

"That was eight years ago. I never thought I'd still be bulimic today. The first person I talked to about my eating disorder was my pastor. He and the elders prayed for me one Sunday morning. For one week I was much better. Then my old habits set in again. I have been to faith healers, retreat centers, and hospitals. I used to blame God even though I knew I wasn't doing my best to change. I guess I wanted Him to fix everything for me.

"I am finally getting better. I have been in counseling for a year and am attending an Overeaters Anonymous support group. I've changed a lot of my bad thinking patterns and have alternatives and friends to turn to when I feel a binge coming on. I'm even learning to like myself, and for the first time in my life I'm able to eat in moderation."

Danielle was not instantaneously healed of her eating disorder. Instead, she had to learn to replace bingeing and purging with moderate eating. As she did, she began to live a moderate lifestyle by God's grace, and was experiencing the truth that God "richly supplies us with everything for our enjoyment" (1 Timothy 6:17).

There is hope! Food can be a moderate part of your life, too. Complete and total restoration is possible. When you're thinking about your own healing, it may help you to know that there are different kinds of healing available. Let's look at two ways restoration can occur.

MIRACLES AND COMMON HEALING

One type of restoration is a miracle. God provides an immediate healing which takes away all cravings and obsessive thoughts about food. If He has done that for you, hallelujah! That is an example of divine healing where God breaks through the barriers of nature to bring about a supernatural change.

Divine healing is what most of us want—and sometimes demand—God to do. When it seems as though our prayers are bouncing off the ceiling and that healing isn't taking place, it's easy to become discouraged and to assume that God isn't interested in helping us. But nothing could be further from the truth.

It is important to remember that God is not locked into our expectations or demands. He says, "As the heavens are higher than the earth, so are my ways higher than your ways and my thoughts than your thoughts" (Isaiah 55:9). In His wisdom, He knows what is best for each individual. I believe that He knows who would most benefit from a gradual healing process. If you have not received an instantaneous deliverance or healing, don't lose heart. You have many biblical, medical, and psychological helps available to integrate with your day-to-day walk with God. As you make an effort to grab and utilize the help that is available, God will help you walk out of slavery into freedom.

Common healing is another way God brings healing into our lives. Many of the methods discussed in this book are means of common healing. If you believe that God has supplied mankind with knowledge in the medical and psychological sciences, then it is logical to assume that He will use sciences to bring healing to His people.

Yes, it does take time to learn how to use these tools, and it requires effort. But in the process, you have the privilege of being involved in a cooperative contract where you and God work together toward restoration.

God wants to bring stability and balance back into your life. He delights in and blesses every step taken to combat deceit. He will honor your honesty about needing help. As you choose not to play games and to take responsibility to do your part in the healing process, God will back you 100 percent. He enthusiastically helps His children move out of disequilibrium and into balanced wholeness.

MEANING IN THE HEALING PROCESS

You may have been struggling with your eating disorder for a long time, and the road to recovery seems very crooked and rocky. I want to encourage you to find meaning and purpose in what you are experiencing. If you do, you will be sustained and strengthened.

Viktor Frankl, the great German psychotherapist, had a successful practice and a loving family which was torn apart when he was placed in a concentration camp in World War II. He lost his home, his family, and his profession. Dr. Frankl lost contact with his wife, suffered a great deal, and watched others die in inhuman conditions. Instead of giving up and dying like others did, he looked for meaning to help him survive. He believed that one of his purposes in life was to help others, and he began to see the opportunity he had while in the middle of a camp of suffering. He didn't stop with the awareness of what he could do; he poured himself into his fellow sufferers.

Dr. Frankl knew that he had been placed on this earth for a reason. Even the concentration camp experience had meaning when he considered how his survival could help others. The spark of God's image in him burned so brightly that no amount of suffering could extinguish life's meaning. Do you have the same hope for meaning while you are in the midst of struggling with your eating disorder?

I'd like to tell you what one of my clients said in group counseling one evening. Her perspective may help you sort through some of your feelings on the subject of healing. "For three years I begged God every night to take away my eating disorder as I cried myself to sleep. I can see now that God answered my prayer by leading me to a Christian counselor who knew about eating disorders. I have been in therapy now for eleven months, and my life has been turned around. I've learned to be honest with myself, with God, and with my family. I've learned to take responsibility for my feelings, and that I can't blame God or others for my problems.

"My eating disorder is coming under control, and one day soon I'm certain that I'll be completely free of it. I'm glad God didn't heal me instantly, because if He had, I would have missed out on everything I've learned over the last eleven months. The person I am on the inside is being healed and that goes much deeper than a physical healing."

Healing is much more than a "quick fix," and suffering brings deep changes and growth. If you are suffering on your way to healing, there can be meaning, purpose, and growth born out of this difficult time. There is hope!

MYTHS ABOUT GETTING WELL

Sometimes a person can be blocked from making progress in the healing process simply because they believe misconceptions about getting well. I've seen this happen so frequently that I thought it would be helpful to mention four of the most common myths that people innocently, but mistakenly, believe.

I must get over my eating disorder on my own. As I mentioned earlier, this is not a healthy perspective, yet I find this myth especially often among evangelical Christians. It is usually coupled with the idea that "God and I need to go it alone." This viewpoint always intrigues me, because nowhere in Scripture are we commanded to "go it alone." Instead, we find the Scriptures demanding interdependency with others. I realize this is totally different than the secular mindset which pushes independence and isolation. But God's ways frequently do not parallel man's ways.

In John 17, just prior to the account of Christ's death and resurrection, Christ prays to God the Father for His disciples and for all other believers. In several of the twenty-six verses in that chapter, He communicates His earnest desire for believers to be united and intimate with one another. "Jesus said this, and looked toward heaven and prayed. . . . I will remain in the world no longer, but they are still in the world, and I am coming to you. Holy Father, protect them by the power of your name—the name you gave me—so that they may be one even as we are one. . . . My prayer is not for them alone [His disciples]. I pray also for those who will believe in me through their message, that all of them may be one, Father, just you are in me and I am in you. May they also be in us so that the world may believe that you have sent me. . . . May they be brought to complete unity to let the world know that you sent me and have loved them even as you have loved me" (John 17:1, 11, 20-22).

God always presses His children toward unity, oneness of mind, and interdependency. The nature of this type of a relationship demands openness, transparency, and vulnerability. God has not asked you to be a Lone Ranger. Don't be duped by the myth that the spiritual thing to do is to go it alone.

I first need to understand all the reasons why I have an eating disorder before I can begin to get well. This second myth is simply not true. Many people recovering from anorexia and bulimia make changes in their eating behavior, and at the same time begin a process of understanding the factors that contribute to their disorder. Usually I hear this myth from individuals who are trying to circumvent their responsibility in the healing process. It's an excuse to cover for their lack of effort in combating their disorder. They think, "Since I don't understand, I can't get well." Out of all of the studies conducted on anorexia and bulimia, I am not aware of any that have supported the above statement. I encourage you to see it for what it really is: a myth that can inhibit your healing.

It will take me years to heal since I have had my eating disorder for years. This is not an accurate understanding of the healing process. I believe that the speed of the healing process is related to how willing you are to 1) take responsibility for your behavior, 2) grab and use the tools available through the sciences of medicine and psychology, and 3) cultivate a personal relationship with God on a daily basis, so that He is intimately a part of your healing and His Word plays an active part in your thoughts.

I have seen individuals who have been bulimic or anorexic for five to ten years overcome their eating disorder in less than a year. Others have taken longer. But those who quickly recover paid a price. They didn't avoid help; they sought it out. They moved out of their comfort zones and took responsibility for their feelings and actions. They grabbed and implemented the coping skills they were taught. Every step of the way they asked God for strength and courage to keep going. Memorized Scriptures encouraged them in the gloomy times, and a support system that they could depend on surrounded them when the going got tough. Yes, they did pay a price. However, they'll be the first to say it was worth it because today they experience freedom.

Be encouraged: the length of your healing process is not determined by the length of time you've been struggling. I firmly believe that you and God are a winning team. With Him, you'll experience a much faster and deeper healing than those who try to "go it alone." Your past failures haven't caught God off guard, nor have they tied His hands. God takes you as you are and is committed to your personal growth as much or more than you are.

The Battle Can Be Won!

Once I have an eating disorder, it will be a part of me for the rest of my life. In other words, "Once a bulimic or anorexic, always a bulimic or anorexic. The battle can't be won." I vehemently disagree with this idea, even though some counseling professionals would argue for it. I suppose the reason I am opposed to this fatalistic perspective is that it leaves absolutely no room for hope or for God to intervene. It leaves the struggling victim deep in despair, wondering, "Why bother to fight it if this disorder will be with me until the grave?"

I would like to counter this myth with truths found in God's Word that document the fact that *the battle can be won.* The truths of the Bible stand the test of time and are able to give hope when you fight against the myth that you cannot experience healing. Be encouraged by God's Word; the battle can be won!

YOU CAN EXPERIENCE HEALING

Of all the tragedies that can happen in life, the forfeiting of hope and the failure to look forward are the worst. You may feel like healing is for others, but not for you. Perhaps your war has gone on for years; you're whipped by battle fatigue, and hopelessness has set in.

If there is one truth I want you to glean from this book, it is this: *You can experience healing!* You don't have to be in bondage to food the rest of your life. How can I say that? Because God is the author of tomorrows and new beginnings. But you have a choice. You can shrink back and hide from tomorrow or you can face tomorrow and say, "OK, God, I don't have all the answers. But I'm going to try my best to win this battle. I'm going to trust you to help me one hour at a time. Regardless of my feelings, I choose today to believe that healing will happen in my life as we work together."

Take a moment now to review some powerful biblical truths that sponsor hope. With God's help you can experience victory.

"I can do all things through Him who strengthens me" (Philippians 4:13 NASB). Many people go through life thinking of Christ as their judge rather than their source of strength. Are you one of these people? Jesus Christ wants to give you the strength, power, and ability to face things victoriously in your life. You may feel that you have to be a winner in your own strength. But the great thing about knowing God is that His resources are yours, and you don't have to win on your own will power. His power will back you!

"If you have faith . . . nothing shall be impossible" (Matthew 17:20 NIV). What do you believe in? Sometimes we put our trust in the wrong places. The word *faith* in the original Greek and Hebrew means "to put one's heart into." Eating disorders can mean having faith in scales, food, and purging. Relearning to put our heart into God's hands or put our faith in Him will help us survive the impossible. While there are no easy answers and there will be failures, we can still trust God with everything, including the outcome of our eating habits.

"God is for us" (Romans 8:31 NASB). No one feels as alone as the person who is hassled by eating disorders. Maybe you're experiencing the sting of aloneness today. It may seem as though everybody is on the opposite side and that God is very far away. But God said, "I will never leave you." Even in the deepest ruts of your eating disorder, God doesn't desert you. Remember that He loves you . . . He is on your side!

God's continual presence is available to you on a moment-by-moment basis. You don't have to walk the recovery road alone. As you invite Him to help you, there is no difficulty or defeat that can't be overcome. You don't have to win the whole war in one day. As you face each individual battle, one at a time, you can experience victory. And with God's help, in time, your war will be won!

APPENDIX: CHARTS

THOUGHT RECORD

Date	Situation	Feeling (s)	Automatic Thoughts	Realistic Answers	Outcome

DATE:

TODAY'S SUCCESS STRATEGY

	TIME	PLACE	FOOD EATEN	CALORIES	THOUGHTS & FEELINGS
Breakfast					
Lunch					
Dinner					
Snacks					
TOTAL					

TOMORROW'S BATTLE PLAN

CALORIES

Breakfast

subtotal:

Lunch

subtotal:

Dinner

subtotal:

Snacks

subtotal:

TOTAL

ADDITIONAL
HELPFUL RESOURCES

ADDITIONAL HELPFUL RESOURCES
Readings on Anorexia Nervosa and Bulimia

Barrile, Jackie. *Confessions of a Closet Eater.* Wheaton, Illinois: Tyndale House, 1983.

Bruch, Hilde. *The Golden Cage: The Enigma of Anorexia Nervosa.* Cambridge, Mass.: Harvard University Press, 1978. (A very readable discussion of causes and treatment, focusing on individual therapy.)

Crisp, A. H. *Anorexia Nervosa: Let Me Be.* New York: Grune and Statton, Inc., 1980.

Landau, Elaine. *Why Are They Starving Themselves?* New York: Julian Messner/Simon & Schuster, 1983.

MacLeod, Sheila. *The Art of Starvation: A Story of Anorexia Nervosa and Survival.* New York: Schocken Books, 1981.

Minuchin, Salvador. *Psychosomatic Families: Anorexia Nervosa in Context.* Cambridge, Mass.: Harvard University Press, 1978. (An excellent, readable presentation of family systems therapy.)

Orbach, Susie. *Fat Is a Feminist Issue.* New York: Berkley Books, 1978.

_____. *Fat Is a Feminist Issue II.* New York: Berkley Books, 1982.

Palmer, R. L. *Anorexia Nervosa: A Guide for Sufferers and Their Families.* New York: Penguin Books, 1980. (A readable overview of etiology, physiological changes, and treatment—written so the lay person can understand.)

Sours, John. *Starving to Death in a Sea of Objects: The Anorexia Nervosa Syndrome.* New York: Jason Aronson, 1978. (A thorough presentation of the psychoanalytic approach to treating anorexia nervosa.)

Squire, Susan. *The Slender Balance.* New York: G. P. Putnam's Sons, 1983.

Vincent, L. M. *Competing with the Sylph: The Pursuit of the Ideal Body Form.* New York: Berkeley Books, 1979. (A book focusing on women's pursuit of thinness, written by a dancer-turned-doctor. Healthy alternatives are suggested.)

White, William C. and Boskind-White, Marlene. *Bulimarexia.* New York: W. W. Norton & Company, 1983.

Books On Related Topics, Not Specifically Anorexia Nervosa or Bulimia

Briggs, Dorothy Corkille. *Your Child's Self-Esteem.* New York: Doubleday & Co., Inc., 1970. (Directed specifically to parents, outlining ways in which self-image and self-esteem are built during childhood, and offering suggestions how parents can help their children develop healthy views of themselves.)

Burns, David D. *Feeling Good.* New York: New American Library, 1981.

Kuntzleman, Charles. *Diet Free: The No-Diet Way to a Beautiful Body.* Emmaus, Pa.: Rodale Press, 1981. (A fresh, intelligent, realistic approach to weight management via a healthy, balanced lifestyle.)

Powell, John. *The Secret of Staying in Love.* Niles, Ill.: Argus Communications, 1974. (A thought-provoking presentation of the essence of unconditional love and intimacy.)

_____. *Why Am I Afraid to Tell You Who I Am?* Niles, Ill: Argus Communications, 1969.

Narramore, Bruce. *You're Someone Special.* Grand Rapids: The Zondervan Corporation, 1980.

Wright, Norman. *Answer to Family Communication.* Eugene, Oreg.: Harvest House, 1977.

Organizations

For help or information on eating disorders, write to the address in your part of the country:

Anorexia Nervosa & Related Eating Disorders, Inc.
P.O. Box 5102
Eugene, Oregon 97405

Anorexia Nervosa and Associated Disorders, Inc.
P.O. Box 271
Highland Park, IL 60035

National Anorexic Aid Society, Inc.
P.O. Box 29461
Columbus, OH 43229

American Anorexia Nervosa Association, Inc.
133 Cedar Lane
Teaneck, New Jersey 07666